Threshold Competitor
A Management Simulation

THRESHOLD COMPETITOR

A MANAGEMENT SIMULATION

SECOND EDITION

PHILIP A. ANDERSON
DAVID A. BEVERIDGE
TIMOTHY W. SCOTT
DAVID L. HOFMEISTER

PRENTICE HALL
Upper Saddle River, New Jersey 07458

Editor-in-Chief: Natalie Anderson
Assistant Editor: Lisamarie Brassini
Editorial Assistant: Christopher Stogdill
Marketing Manager: Stephanie Johnson
Production Editor: Judith Leale
Managing Editor: Dee Josephson
Manufacturing Buyer: Diane Peirano
Manufacturing Supervisor: Arnold Vila
Manufacturing Manager: Vincent Scelta
Cover Design: Bruce Kenselaar

Copyright © 1998 by Prentice-Hall, Inc.
A Simon & Schuster Company
Upper Saddle River, New Jersey 07458

All rights reserved. No part of this book may be reproduced, in any form or by any means, without written permission from the Publisher.

ISBN 0-13-675539-9

Prentice-Hall International (UK) Limited, London
Prentice-Hall of Australia Pty. Limited, Sydney
Prentice-Hall Canada, Inc., Toronto
Prentice-Hall Hispanoamericana, S.A., Mexico
Prentice-Hall of India Private Limited, New Delhi
Prentice-Hall of Japan, Inc., Tokyo
Simon & Schuster Asia Pte. Ltd., Singapore
Editora Prentice-Hall do Brasil, Ltda., Rio de Janeiro

Printed in the United States of America

10 9 8 7 6 5 4 3 2 1

TABLE OF CONTENTS

Preface vii

Chapter 1 – Overview 1
    What is *Threshold*? 1
    Purposes of *Threshold* 1
    How to Approach the Simulation 2
    Tips on Succeeding with *Threshold* 2
    How to Use This Manual 3

Chapter 2 – Review of Management Functions 5
    Planning 5
        Mission Statement 6
        Statement of Goals 7
        Strategies and Policies 7
        Other Planning Activities 8
    Organizing and Staffing 8
    Leading 9
    Controlling 10

Chapter 3 – The *Threshold* Business Environment 11
    Your Company's Products 11
    History of Your Company 11
    Current Status of Your Company 12
    Your Company's Marketplace 13

Chapter 4 – Using the Company Disk 15
    Chapter Overview 15
    What You Need 15
        Computer System Requirements 15
        Other Needs 16
    Navigating Around *Threshold* 16
        Using a Mouse vs. No Mouse 16
        Using the PgUp and PgDn Keys 16
        Using the "Hot" Keys 16
    The Company Disk 16
    Starting the *Threshold* Program 17
        Start Your Computer 17
        Using the DOS Version of *Threshold* 18
        <u>Setting Up</u> the Windows Version of *Threshold* 18
        <u>Using</u> the Windows Version of *Threshold* 20
    The Initial Time You Start the *Threshold* Program 20
        Entering a Company Name 21
        Entering a Password 21
    The *Threshold* Program 21
    Entering a Decision 22
    Saving Your Decisions 23
    Correcting an Error 23

Moving the Cursor Around *Threshold's* Decision Screens 23
    Using the Tab Key 23
    Using the Mouse 23
Moving From Screen to Screen 24
    Using the PgUp and PgDn Keys 24
    Using the Menu Bar 26
    Using *Threshold's* "Hot" Keys 28
Menu Bar Operations 28
    The File Menu 28
    The Decision Menu 30
    The Reports Menu 31
    The Info Menu 32
    The Print Menu 33
Seeing the *Forecasted* Results of Your Decisions 35
Seeing the *Actual* Results of Earlier Quarters 36
Using a Hard Disk 36
Making a Backup Disk 38
    Making a Backup Disk Using DOS Commands 39
    Making a Backup Disk Using Windows 39
Trouble Shooting 39
    Complete System Failure 40
    Threshold Program Failure 40
    Viruses 40
    Data Entry Errors 40
Re-Process a Previous Quarter 40

Chapter 5 – Making Decisions 43
Overview of Decisions 43
The Business Plan 43
    Developing a Business Plan 43
Marketing Decisions 44
    Price 44
    Television Advertisements 45
    Newspaper Advertisements 45
    Magazine Advertisements 45
Sales Forecast Estimate 45
Market Research Decisions 47
    Price by Company 47
    Television, Newspaper, Magazine and Product Quality Reports 47
    Units Sold by Company 48
    Future Sales Potential 48
Production Decisions 49
    Buy Raw Materials 49
    Investment in Product Quality 49
    Number of Units to Produce 50
    Workers to Hire, Fire, Lay Off 51
    Buy or Sell Plant Capacity 52
    Human Resource Development 53
Finance Decisions 54
    Short-Term Loans 54

Long-Term Mortgages 55
Short-Term Investments 55
Management Dilemmas 56
Cost Parameters Report 56

Chapter 6 – *Threshold* Reports 58
Operations Reports 58
Inventory Reports 58
Labor Report 60
Cost of Production 61
Selling and Administrative Expense Report 63
Income Statement 64
Balance Sheet 66
Assets 67
Liabilities 67
Owners' Equity 68
Cash Flow Statement 68
Industry Performance Report 71

Appendix A – Quarter 0 Decisions 74
Appendix B – Quarter 0 Reports 75
Appendix C – Sample Market Research Report for a Three Team Industry 79
Appendix D – Initial Cost Parameters 80
Appendix E – *Threshold* Limits and Time Lags 81
Appendix F – *Threshold* "Hot" Keys 82
Appendix G – Management Dilemmas 83
    1. Why Does It Have To Be Emily? 84
    2. Can You Steal Garbage? 85
    3. The Older Employee 87
    4. The Alcoholic Employee 88
    5. Wildcat Strike 89
    6. The Substitute Raw Materials 90
    7. Where There's Smoke There's Fire. 91
    8. Did You Hear the One About ...? 93
Appendix H – Sample Industry Performance Report 95
Appendix I – Company Decision Worksheet 96
Appendix J – Flow Chart of *Threshold* Decisions 97

Index 98

PREFACE

WHAT IS *THRESHOLD*?

Threshold is a computer program that simulates the workings of a small business. You use *Threshold* as a member of a group to make the decisions needed to run a small manufacturing business. Each group manages separate companies, which are all in competition with each other in the same marketplace. The companies are not in competition with the computer. The computer's function is just to process your decisions quickly and to provide reports that show the results of those decisions.

In *Threshold*, you:
- act as the management team for your company, deciding on a company mission, goals, policies, and strategies
- develop skills in planning, organizing, staffing, directing, and controlling a business
- make decisions in the areas of:
    1. marketing, including market research and sales forecasts
    2. finance, including short-term and long-term loans
    3. manufacturing, including raw materials, production, scheduling, staffing, and inventory control
- have the opportunity to ask "what-if" questions by entering a sales estimate and seeing what the results of your decisions would be given this level of sales
- see the results of your decisions and have an opportunity to correct mistakes in the following quarters of operation

WHAT ARE THE BENEFITS OF *THRESHOLD*?

- *Threshold* allows you to put into practice the principles of management that you have learned in an introductory business course.
- It allows you to see the interrelationships of the various areas of a business, so you see how production and marketing decisions, for example, impact the financial area.
- It makes financial statements meaningful as you see how your decisions impact on your income statement and balance sheet.
- *Threshold* allows you to input decisions directly on a computer, rather than put decisions on input sheets that have to be entered by someone else with the possibility of error. The computer program also checks each input to be sure it is within the allowable range.
- It gives you the opportunity to work in a group to develop and work toward mutual goals.

WHAT ARE THE COMPUTER SYSTEM REQUIREMENTS?

You will need to have access to a personal computer with the following characteristics.

If you are using the DOS version of *Threshold*, your computer must have:
- 640K of memory (1 Meg is preferred).
- at least 1 disk drive.
- monochrome or color monitor.
- printer (optional).

If you are using the Windows version of *Threshold*, your computer must have:
- 4 Meg of memory with Windows 3.1 (8 Meg is preferred if using Windows 95).
- 1 Meg of space on your hard disk.
- at least 1 disk drive.
- monochrome or color monitor.
- printer (optional).

HOW DOES *THRESHOLD* WORK?

You work on a personal computer, entering decisions on two screens. You can review previous quarters' decisions and results either on the screen or on printouts as you work.

When your decisions for a quarter of *Threshold* operations are final, the disks are handed into the administrator. The administrator then processes the decisions, using the *Threshold* Administrator program. The *Threshold* program determines the number of products each company sold and also produces a series of operations, marketing, and financial reports for each company. The program also rates the teams and ranks them according to criteria determined by the administrator.

ACKNOWLEDGMENTS

We would like to thank the following people for their help and contributions to *Threshold*. As always, our families deserve thanks for their patience as we took time from them to work on this project. To Sue, Lona, Emily, and Kelly – Thanks.

We also would like to thank the participants and faculty (Ron Klocke, Richard Paulson, and Miles Smayling) at Mankato State University for participating in the class testing of this 2nd edition of *Threshold*. We would also like to thank Gaber Abou Elenein, Dean of the College of Business at Mankato State University, for his help and support of this project. A special note of gratitude goes to Vivekanand (Vivek) Addagudi for his tireless crunching of the numbers to test the accuracy of our code and to Paul Schumann for his exhaustive edit of this manual. We would like to thank Leigh Lawton at the University of St. Thomas for his insights and assistance in developing *Threshold's* marketing model. We also want to acknowledge the students at the University of St. Thomas who participated in the class testing of *Threshold*.

We want to thank Jill Purdy at the University of Washington, Tacoma who coordinated an off-site beta test for us. Jill, her colleagues, and the students at UW Tacoma provided invaluable feedback that improved both the software and the manual. We would also like to extend thanks to Lou Harmin. Lou cared enough about this project to read the manuals and provide fresh feedback as a user of the 1st edition. Lou, most importantly, introduced Dave to Phil and Tim.

A special note about our friend Dave Hofmeister, who designed and created the 1st Edition *Threshold* software. Dave died suddenly of a heart attack in December 1993. We owe much to his dedication and determination to provide a product for you that would combine education, learning, and fun. As we worked on the new edition, we felt his presence. His spirit lives with us and in the code of this product. We hope that Dave approves of what we did with his "baby."

P.H.A.
D.A.B.
T.W.S.

CHAPTER 1

OVERVIEW

WHAT IS *THRESHOLD COMPETITOR*?

Threshold Competitor (hereafter just called *Threshold*) is a computer-based model that simulates a small business. Your assignment is to manage *Threshold's* operations. You will act as one member of a team of top-level managers of a small manufacturing company, making decisions about all aspects of the business. This will involve making decisions regarding production and marketing of your products. It will also include decisions about financing the costs of your marketing and production operations. Your team will compete with other teams that are managing other companies selling similar products in your industry's marketplace. The computer will process your team's decisions and those of the other companies and provide reports on how well each company did. The computer will determine how many sales each company made and provide operations, marketing, and financial reports on the company. The teams will manage their companies for several quarters, analyzing the results of each quarter to help them make decisions for the next quarter's operations.

When managing your *Threshold* company, you are not in competition with the computer. Instead, your competitors are other teams who are working on the simulation. The computer's function is only to process the companies' decisions and provide reports that show the results of those decisions.

The *Threshold* program contains mathematical formulas and sets of rules. These formulas and rules allow the program to simulate, or imitate, the results that a business decision would have in the real world. So, for example, the *Threshold* program can determine how a company's sales would be affected by the price that it sets for its product when compared with the prices of its competitors' products.

Threshold was designed to help you understand the practice of management and to improve your personal skills in managing an enterprise. *Threshold* will be challenging, but manageable. It will make topics you read in a management textbook or cover in a management class more real and, consequently, more understandable. It will give you a chance to put into practice what you have learned in your business studies, and to see the results of your actions. The chance to test out your ideas is one of the best ways for you to learn about the field of management. *Threshold* provides you with this opportunity.

PURPOSES OF *THRESHOLD*

Working with the *Threshold* simulation will help you to:
- understand the importance of a business plan in guiding business decisions,
- develop skills in planning, organizing, staffing, directing, and controlling a business,
- acquire personal experiences that will help you to understand the issues presented in an introductory management course,
- understand the relationships between financial statements such as the cash flow statement, the income statement, and the balance sheet,
- understand the relationships between marketing, operations, and finance, and
- understand the operational issues of production, inventory, plant and work-force use, and scheduling.

HOW TO APPROACH THE SIMULATION

Management is a blend of art and science. This means the process of managing requires working with both the facts of the situation you are facing and with your intuition of how to succeed in that environment. Emphasizing one of these at the expense of the other makes a manager less effective. Intuitive problem-solvers make decisions without considering all of the data available to them. They are more concerned with their "gut feelings" than with the realities they face. Ignoring these realities results in decisions that are ineffective in resolving the problem being faced. By contrast, problem-solvers who rely completely on facts tend not to consider the aspects of a problem that cannot be easily reduced to numbers. Certainly, not everything that contributes to the resolution of a particular problem can be quantified. This approach, then, also leaves out key components of a problem's solution. *Threshold* will give you a chance to develop and practice both kinds of managerial thinking. While you must work with the numbers generated in your *Threshold* reports, you must also get a feel for the simulated business environment *Threshold* creates. Learning to manage both of these dimensions of a problem will make you a more effective manager, not only of your *Threshold* company, but also in subsequent business experiences you encounter.

Many college participants dislike working in a group. They feel that it is not like work in "the real world." In fact, groups working on *Threshold* face almost exactly the same problems that a work group in any business organization has to face. Managers do much of their work in a business organization in teams. Working with a group of individuals requires learning how to manage competing individual ideas and egos while successfully accomplishing the group's goal. This is a common experience in the modern organization. It is also a necessary element in successfully managing the *Threshold* simulation. In business, as in the *Threshold* simulation, each participant's knowledge, motivation, determination, and time available to devote to the circumstances faced, affects the success of the enterprise. Learning to work together, cooperatively, as peers, is a critical ingredient for success in any business enterprise.

TIPS ON SUCCEEDING WITH *THRESHOLD*

The following are some tips to help you when you are working with the *Threshold* simulation:

- <u>Manage your time efficiently</u>. Learning how to manage time is a primary concern for any manager. It affects success in any business. There will never be enough time to do all that you would wish to do. Being able to determine what issues to focus on (setting priorities) and to stay focused on these issues (efficiency) will have a significant impact on the effectiveness of the decisions you make. Working with a group on *Threshold* gives you practice at managing this critical resource. Developing good time-management skills will increase your chances of success in your business career.

- <u>Manage your business, do not guess at your decisions</u>. *Threshold* teams can either manage their company or guess when making decisions regarding the future of their company. Managing the business involves having company goals, plus plans and strategies for meeting those goals. These goals, plans, and strategies are used to guide a team's decision making. Guessing leads to making decisions randomly and without any consistency over time. This may be easier and more fun in the short run. You may even initially get better results than your competition. However, in the long run, teams who make their decisions by guessing will not be able to outperform teams who make their decisions carefully. This is because you will not understand what you did that was correct and what you need to change to improve your position in subsequent quarters. Nor will you be sensitive to changes that your competitors are making or to changes in your general economic climate. *Threshold* is the kind of project where the more effort you put into it, the more you get out of it.

- Learn from your failures as well as your successes. Managers must always deal with their own and others' mistakes. When your decisions in *Threshold* do not give you the results you planned for, nor are they satisfactory for the long-term success of your company, analyze the results to see what you should do differently next time. A successful manager learns how to capitalize on success, recover from mistakes, and move forward to improve the company's position. You can often learn more from what you do wrong than from what you do right.
- Do not worry if you are confused at first. Participants are often confused when they begin working with *Threshold*. Remember, this is most likely a new form of learning experience for you. Working with a simulation requires *applying* your knowledge and skills to a business operation rather than *listening* to a lecture about the knowledge and skills needed to operate the business. It is a fundamental change from hearing to doing.

    As with any new experience, it can be confusing and a bit overwhelming at first. However, after you make two or three sets of decisions, you should feel familiar with the rules of the simulation and more comfortable with learning through active application rather than passive listening. Remember, your competitors are facing the same confusion that you are experiencing. Consequently, your willingness to invest the effort to learn your new environment quicker than your competition will have a significant impact on your ability to out-perform your competition.

    This also replicates what you will experience in the world of business. Managers face a constantly changing business environment. Their ability to understand quickly this new business situation significantly affects their personal and organizational success. You have only to think about the changes in computer technology you have witnessed over the past few years to recognize the importance of being able to adjust to changes around you.

HOW TO USE THIS MANUAL

Read this manual thoroughly, but do not try to memorize it. Instead, read to get a sense of the business environment created by the simulation. Then, as you work on *Threshold*, refer to the appropriate sections of the manual for specific information. You will notice that the simulation's program contains much of the information supplied by this manual. For example, you can access the costs of operating the business and the timing sequences between events (i.e., time lags between when you make your decisions and when you will experience the results of these decisions) through the Menu Bar in the program. We will explain how to do this later in this manual.

When you get to Chapter 4, you will want to begin using the *Threshold* disk on your computer. Learning how to use the disk and keyboard to enter and record your decisions will make the rest of the manual easier to understand.

The appendices have a number of forms and exhibits to help you manage your company. Glance over these as you read the manual and refer to them later when you need the information.

This is what is covered in the remaining chapters of this manual:
- Chapter 2 reviews the fundamentals of management and shows how this simulation reflects these fundamentals.
- Chapter 3 describes the company you will manage and the business environment in which you will operate.
- Chapter 4 introduces you to the computer and to the simulation model created by *Threshold*'s programs. It gives you a quick "guided tour" of the simulation.

- Chapter 5 covers the decisions you will make and tells you how to enter them on the computer and consequently onto your company disk.
- Chapter 6 describes the reports you will receive after each team makes decisions for each quarter of operation and after the computer has processed those decisions.
- Appendix A shows the decisions made in the last quarter of operations just prior to your team taking over the management of the company.
- Appendix B includes reports of the results of the decisions shown in Appendix A.
- Appendix C is an example of the market research reports you can purchase to help you in making decisions in future quarters, as you continue to manage your company.
- Appendix D provides a listing of the initial cost parameters for various elements in *Threshold*, such as advertising rates, costs for market research, and interest rates for loans and investments. This appendix also includes the worker productivity in Quarter 1 for each of the two products that your company produces. These costs and productivity levels will most certainly change during your management of your *Threshold* company. Current costs and productivity levels will be on your company disk. Directions for accessing current cost information through the menu bar in the *Threshold* program will be explained in Chapter 4.
- Appendix E gives you some important limits on the decisions you can make in the management of your *Threshold* company. For example, it tells you the range of prices you are allowed to charge for your products. You can also access this information through the menu bar in the *Threshold* program. We will explain this later in the manual (See Chapter 4).
- Appendix F gives the screens to which you can move directly using *Threshold*'s "hot" keys. These are a combination of the CTRL, Shift, and Function (e.g., F1) keys. Directions for using these "hot" keys are given in Chapter 4.
- Appendix G describes some management dilemmas that your company may face during your management of the simulation. These dilemmas represent managerial problems outside your company's normal operations. Making decisions regarding *Threshold*'s management dilemmas is discussed in Chapter 5.
- Appendix H is an example of an Industry Performance Report. It shows how each company did in sales, income, return on sales, and sales forecasting when compared to the performance of the other companies in the simulation.
- Appendix I is a blank decision form to use for recording the decisions you make each quarter. Each quarter's decisions that you make will be saved on your company's disk.
- Appendix J provides a flow chart of the decisions you will make and how they lead to forecast and actual reports you will use to manage your *Threshold* company.

CHAPTER 2

REVIEW OF MANAGEMENT FUNCTIONS

The purpose of this chapter is to review the functions of management and show how each of these is involved in your management of the *Threshold* simulation.

Management is the process of establishing goals for an organization and then working effectively and efficiently to achieve those goals. Effective managers attain their goals. Efficient managers achieve those goals without wasting resources. For example, they manufacture the desired number of products at the lowest possible cost. Effectiveness is concerned with the accomplishment of goals. Efficiency is concerned with using the minimal amount of resources to accomplish those goals. An effective manager cares whether the goals are reached. An efficient manager is concerned with getting there for the least possible cost.

It is important for a manager to be both effective *and* efficient. For example, a manager might succeed at selling a desired quantity of a product (i.e., the manager was effective). However, if excessive overtime was needed in order to produce enough of the product to meet the high sales goal, the cost of manufacturing the product could also become excessive. The net result could be losses and a failed business. Similarly, a manager may succeed in cutting costs, but cut them so severely that the company fails to sell enough to be profitable. For example, reducing advertising will save on those expenses, but also will reduce sales as fewer people are aware of what your products have to offer them. Drawing the proper balance between effectiveness and efficiency is the mark of a successful manager.

The functions of management are interrelated activities managers perform to achieve their chosen goals. Most textbooks say that managers plan, organize, staff, lead, and control. Each of these managerial functions can be further broken down into smaller parts. For example, planning has the following elements:
- formulating objectives (what you want to achieve);
- formulating strategies and policies (what behavior you will use to pursue your goals);
- problem solving (developing alternative actions for overcoming obstacles to achieving your goals);
- decision making (choosing which alternatives to implement).

PLANNING

Planning is the most basic management function. It should be the first function your team performs when you begin *Threshold*. Planning is deciding in advance what to do, how to do it, when to do it, who is to do it, and where it will be done. Planning comes first because you cannot, for example, determine the financial needs for your company's activities until you know what you want to accomplish. The financing (i.e., money) needed to manage a large-scale company is considerably different from that needed to operate a small, niche player in the industry.

Planning is costly in its use of resources, especially time. Often groups do not like to plan, arguing that things change too fast to make planning worth the effort. While excessive planning can be inefficient, making decisions without a plan is also inefficient when the company has to correct mistakes made because it had no clear sense of direction. For example, a company must know whether it wants to offer a high-quality/high-priced product or a low-quality/low-priced product *before* it can determine decisions regarding production volume and advertising. Your team must balance the benefits and costs associated with formulating and operating a plan. Remember also that planning is an ongoing process, not a one-time event. Just because the team develops a plan at the beginning of the simulation does not mean planning activities are finished. You will need to adjust your goals and policies in response to your competitors' actions and to unforeseen changes in your environment. This means your company should periodically reevaluate its plan and make adjustments to reflect current conditions.

Mission Statement

The first step in the planning process for *Threshold*, as it should be for any company, is the development of a company mission. A mission statement describes the purpose of the organization. It states why your company is in business and what kind of company it wants to be. Identifying a mission is critical to guiding your business successfully. Without this focus to guide your decision making, you may drift in how you approach your marketplace. As a consequence, the competitors who have a clearer mission will enjoy more success than you. They will know who their customer is and be ahead of you in determining what that customer wants.

The focus of a mission statement should be on the marketplace in which the company plans to operate. Who are the customers that it wants to serve? What customer need does the company intend to fulfill? And how will the company satisfy that need better than its competitors? The core of a mission statement should not be about making a profit, but about satisfying a customer need. This does not mean that making a profit is not important. A company wants and needs to be as profitable as possible if it is to maintain a long-term existence. If a company cannot sustain a profitable operation, it will eventually go out of business. If it can't achieve a level of profit which allows it to invest in the future, it will lose its ability to compete in the marketplace over time as others invest in product enhancements and cost-effective equipment. Consequently, knowing where a company wants to go becomes key to knowing where, and in what, to invest the profits of today's operations. Further, understanding what customer needs you are trying to satisfy is critical to knowing how to allocate the company's limited resources.

Which of these, satisfying a customer need or making a profit, is the principle purpose of a business? Which of these should come first? That is the classic chicken-egg conundrum. Clearly, you must attend to both. Our belief is that you should start with the desire to satisfy a need, recognizing that if you do not maintain a profitable organization, your ability to satisfy that need will be short lived. If a company does not make a profit, it can not continue to satisfy its customers' needs, no matter how much its customers may want what the company is offering them. Consequently, we contend that a company has an obligation to make a profit so that it can continue to satisfy the needs of its customers and pay its employees a fair wage.

The debate may be less on whether making a profit is acceptable, but more on how much profit a company should make. At what point does a company begin to "gouge" its customers and violate its social responsibility as a corporate citizen? That debate is not the focus of this manual, but you may choose to reflect on the ability of a competitive market to "control" excess profit taking by companies in that market as you participate in the *Threshold* simulation exercise.

A mission statement should not consist simply of a series of platitudes that carry little operational meaning, such as "to maximize profits." The mission statement needs to go beyond statements of profitability in order to give the organization identity and focus, both for yourself and for your potential customers. Because you will know very little about your company and its market environment when you begin, your mission statement will be relatively vague compared to that of a real organization. However, you do need to determine, in a broad sense, what role your company will play within its industry. How will you compete with the other teams in the simulation? For example, do you want to be a discount-priced/high-volume producer or a premium-priced/low-volume producer? What will be your competitive edge? How will customers distinguish your company from your competitors' companies? What will you do better than your competition? Perhaps most importantly, why will consumers want to buy your product rather than your competitors'? A sample mission statement is provided in Exhibit 2.1.

EXHIBIT 2.1

SAMPLE MISSION STATEMENT

Our mission is to provide quality-sensitive customers with technologically-advanced, premium products. Our quality focus will extend beyond our products to our employees. We will provide them with a high quality of work life by conducting developmental training programs and maintaining a rewarding compensation structure.

Statement of Goals

Once you determine your company's mission, your team must decide what goals it wants to achieve in order to accomplish that mission. State your goals in terms that provide you with a clear sense of direction. A goal such as "to increase profits" is too vague to be very useful. Goals should also refer to a single, specific topic that is measurable, such as a sales goal or a cost of manufacturing goal. Unless you are able to measure your progress toward a goal, you will be unable to perform the managerial function of control. Control, which we discuss below, involves deciding whether changes are necessary in order to reach your goals. Finally, goals should be challenging but achievable. If you set goals too low, the company will not advance as fast as it could. At the same time, if goals are unreasonably high, people will give up rather than strive to achieve them. Exhibit 2.2 shows some sample goals.

EXHIBIT 2.2

SAMPLE COMPANY GOALS

1. Maintain market share of 25% for both products.
2. Rank in the top 20% of the industry on product quality.
3. Eliminate lost sales due to insufficient inventory levels.
4. Keep manufacturing cost of goods sold below $42.00 for Product 2.
5. Achieve 5% return on sales on a yearly basis.

Strategies and Policies

Once you have set your goals, you must plan how you will achieve them. This involves determining strategies, policies, procedures, and budgets. Strategies identify general courses of action for achieving your goals. Some examples of strategy statements are shown in Exhibit 2.3. Policies specify desired, acceptable behavior within your organization and serve as the basis for controlling behavior. Procedures and budgets describe the detailed actions you will take and the financial limits within which you will work.

> **EXHIBIT 2.3**
>
> **SAMPLE STRATEGY STATEMENTS**
>
> 1. Utilize premium pricing and advertising to discriminate our product from our competitors' and to finance continued product development.
> 2. Maintain price levels $1.00 above the industry average.
> 3. Invest 7% of sales revenues for Product 1 in quality improvements for that product.
> 4. Maintain safety stock levels at 12% of forecasted sales.
> 5. Maintain work-force levels sufficient to avoid any overtime charges.

Other Planning Activities

Besides developing these broad plans, the team will need to make specific plans in the functional areas of the simulation. For example, *Threshold* requires financial planning. You will need to borrow and repay money needed to operate and perhaps expand the business. In *Threshold*, companies pay out cash immediately for marketing and production expenses. You must pay advertisers and employees at the same time that you use their services. At the same time, each *Threshold* company sells its products on credit, allowing customers to receive the product now, but pay for it later. It takes two quarters to collect all the cash owed for items sold. This delay in receiving payment for your sales, while having to pay immediately for the cost of producing and marketing your product, complicates the need for cash. Your financial planning must take into account the need to pay for the cost of generating sales before you can collect on those sales.

You also are responsible for planning production levels, marketing strategies, and market research activities. Production planning involves forecasting material and labor needs, determining production levels, product quality, and investments in plant expansion. When planning your marketing strategy, you will need to determine how much of the market you intend to capture and what mix of pricing, advertising, and product quality you will use to capture it. You must also decide what market research information you need in order to stay aware of market conditions; i.e., your competitors' actions and predicted future consumer demand levels for products in your industry. Chapter 5 discusses these decisions in more detail.

ORGANIZING AND STAFFING

Once your team has developed a set of plans, you must decide how to organize your group so that you can effectively and efficiently work together to achieve your company's goals. The team should begin by establishing a structure for managing the company. To do this, first develop an organizational chart and a hierarchy of command that clarifies the relationships between the activities needed to manage your company. For example, you may choose to have positions in marketing, operations, and finance; all with a reporting responsibility to a Chief Executive Officer (CEO) who will resolve disputes between individuals in those positions. Next, establish the necessary personal and professional relationships between team members. Remember, you are all entering into this exercise as student peers. You would be well advised to discuss, in advance, how you will manage your dual roles of student (social - friendship) and *Threshold* manager (organizational - work). Then determine the qualifications for each position and the corresponding responsibilities. Finally, the team should staff the company by determining who should fill the positions. Notice that the positions and their duties are determined before the group decides which member will staff which position. This will help you determine whether you need additional skills beyond those the group currently possesses, to effectively manage your company. For example, there may be no one in your group with experience in finance. This will require some outside learning by whoever is assigned to that position, so that he or she can perform the necessary duties of a finance manager. This, too, is no different from what occurs in a business organization. Companies hire people for their ability to learn to manage the responsibilities assigned to them, not just for what they know when they join the organization.

Some company teams will try to "manage" the simulation as a mob. The teams that have established a chain of command and have specialized their efforts will generally perform better. Mobs tend to take a narrow view of the simulation, collectively looking at issues with a single point of view rather than analyzing these issues from a variety of perspectives. Similarly, they often focus on only one issue, rather than seeing the multiplicity of issues that are affecting their company. Organized groups, because of the specialization of individual group members, tend to keep a broader focus on all of their company's activities. This approach allows the group to spot more readily the areas where problems are developing and efficiency can be improved.

LEADING

Your team must decide how it will influence its members to accomplish desired goals. How are you going to divide responsibilities among the team members? Are you going to have a management hierarchy or are you going to operate as a cooperative of equals? Just how are you going to manage your company?

Most likely the members of your team will have a mix of attitudes and abilities. This diversity means that most teams will face some motivational problems as these differences surface during the simulation. Team members may have differing perceptions on what constitutes an acceptable level of effort. One individual may only be willing to put in the effort necessary to receive a "C" for the exercise, while others may want to work at a higher level of effort. The team will have to decide how to deal with an unmotivated or undermotivated group member. The experience of having to work with real problems in motivation is valuable and underlines the fact that not all people choose to perform at the level you want or expect. This is the simulation's equivalent of the leadership function. In real businesses, leaders direct, delegate, coordinate, motivate, manage personal differences, and manage change. You will have to work with all of these issues as you manage your simulation company.

Leading is not always performed in a hierarchical sense. Many organizations rely on teams consisting of individuals from various departments across the company to manage a specific project to its successful completion. Companies also expect employees to work "horizontally" across the organization to accomplish their assigned responsibilities. For example, in order for a marketing person to be effective, he or she must have the cooperation of individuals in the operations area of the business. Failure to manage this relationship will eventually lead to failures in the marketing area.

Further, organizations depend not just on their formal leaders to direct, motivate, and coordinate a group's activities. Informal leaders also play a critical role in an organization's success. Regardless of who is "in charge" of your group, you are all responsible for leading it to a successful experience with *Threshold*. This exercise will give you good experience at managing peers, a critical skill for success in any organization.

CONTROLLING

Finally, your team must deal with issues of control. You must establish a reporting system that determines when and how to obtain information necessary to managing your company. You must also develop performance standards. This means your team needs to determine what indicates good performance by your management team. By monitoring these indicators, you can determine when performance of key duties needs to be improved. Since you can not measure everything, you need to select indicators that are critical to your company's success. Watch these indicators to determine how much your company's actual performance differs from the performance your team desires. For example, you may determine that controlling manufacturing costs is a key to the success of your business. You must then also decide what is the desired manufacturing cost you would like to maintain and what is the maximum cost you can incur without becoming unprofitable. Knowing these numbers will allow you to determine whether you need to take corrective action and where to focus your efforts, should the need arise.

Whether the differences between actual and desired performance require corrective action or not depends on the level of importance your team has given to the indicator and the degree of accuracy desired. If the differences are small, it may not be worthwhile to take action to correct your performance. For example, suppose your team has a goal of no stockouts of Product 1, but also wants to control inventory costs. In order to achieve that goal, you have set a target of maintaining a "safety stock" of 1,000 units of finished goods inventory for Product 1 and stated that a deviation of 500 from that target is acceptable. If you incur an ending inventory of 1,250, you will not have to take any special actions during the next quarter. However, if your ending inventory for Product 1 rises to 1,800 units, corrective action is necessary. The team will have to adjust its activities in order to get its operations back within acceptable performance limits. The ability to identify critical indicators, determine a means for monitoring them, and then adjust decisions to bring the company back in line can easily separate the winners from the also-rans.

The next chapter will provide a description of *Threshold*'s business environment. It will describe your company's history leading up to your team taking managerial control. It will also describe your company's products and its manufacturing capacity, as well as the marketplace in which it operates.

CHAPTER 3

THE *THRESHOLD* BUSINESS ENVIRONMENT

In the *Threshold* simulation, each team is assigned the task of managing a small manufacturing company. All companies start from an identical position. When the simulation exercise begins, each company is in exactly the same financial position. This means each company has the same amount of cash and other assets, as well as the same amount of debt and owners' equity. In addition, each company also has the same inventory, plant capacity, number of production employees, and the same company history. After the first quarter, all of that will change as a consequence of the decisions the teams make. The *Threshold* companies all manufacture the same kinds of products, and compete against each other for customers. So, after the first quarter, companies will have different market shares and will be in different financial positions. Whether your company develops a stronger position relative to the other companies in your industry will depend on your team's ability to manage your company better than competing teams are able to manage their companies.

This chapter describes your company's history and the nature of its business. As you read, keep in mind that you are reading the description of the current position of Company 1, Company 2, or whatever company to which you have been assigned.

YOUR COMPANY'S PRODUCT

In the *Threshold* simulation, you will operate a small manufacturing firm that produces two plastic molded products – Product 1 and Product 2. The manufacturing process consists of forming plastic raw materials (sheets of plastic) into the finished consumer product. You will sell these products through retail markets to the general public. The products are not substitutes for one another, nor are they complementary. This means that sales of one product do not effect sales of the other product.

Given the inherent durability of your products, the likelihood of immediate repeat purchases by a customer is small. This means if a customer has just purchased one of your products in Quarter 1, that customer is not likely to purchase another one in Quarter 2. Consequently, you should assume that sales for a particular quarter will come from new customers that you have attracted to your product based on that quarter's marketing efforts and product characteristics. You should not assume that customers will buy your product because of past experiences with that product. In addition, your company is too new to the market to expect brand satisfaction with one of your products to boost the sales of your other product. In short, each quarter's sales have to be earned that quarter. Brand loyalty is not part of your sales environment.

HISTORY OF YOUR COMPANY

David and Emily Anderscott were the original developers of this business. They and a small group of investors provided the financing needed to establish the company. Your company is privately held because the investors chose not to offer stock for sale to the general public. Neither David, Emily, nor any other owner/investor has any interest in managing the firm. They consider themselves to be financiers rather than managers. Consequently, they have decided to hire a management team from outside the firm to run the business and have selected your team for the job. Your team will have a free hand in managing the company as you best see fit to do. However, the firm's owners expect high performance and will receive quarterly reports that will compare your team's performance with the other management teams operating companies in your industry. If you fail to achieve the success the owners of your company want, they will undoubtedly take action to protect their investment.

Your firm's owners do not freely distribute information about their investments. As a consequence, management reports for two quarters ago, when the company was created, are not available to you. You will receive only the reports for last quarter, Quarter 0, which was the first quarter the company was in operation. These reports are shown in Appendix B. The owners have informed you that, before Quarter 0 (that is, two quarters ago), they were busy setting up the company. They purchased a plant with 11,100 units of production capacity for $499,500. They also hired 45 production workers and purchased 6,500 units of raw materials for Product 1 and 5,500 units of raw material for Product 2 during that quarter. This allowed them to have the necessary plant, labor, and materials for their company to be in operation in Quarter 0. (The results of all these actions are reflected in the Appendix B, Quarter 0 Reports.) In order to finance these activities, the owners put up $249,500 of their money and obtained a mortgage for $250,000 to purchase their plant. A short-term loan paid for that period's purchase of raw materials, the cost of hiring the workers, and general office expenses.

CURRENT STATUS OF YOUR COMPANY

Your company's manufacturing plant is capable of producing 11,100 units of finished product during each quarter of operation (i.e., three months of operation or one quarter of a year). Your production equipment can produce both product lines interchangeably. This allows you to produce both products in the same plant. You are limited in how much you can produce in a particular quarter by three factors: (a) the supply of raw material in inventory for each product, (b) the company's total manufacturing capacity, and (c) the number of production workers on staff to meet those needed for the production level you desire. The plant can produce any combination of your two products. This means that in any one quarter you could, for example, produce 5,000 units of Product 1 and 6,100 units of Product 2. Or you could produce 4,100 of one product and 7,000 of the other. As long as you have the needed raw materials and production labor force, you can produce any combination of the two products that totals 11,100.

You can also produce a limited amount of product at overtime rates. The maximum overtime production allowed is 50% above your normal plant capacity. At your current capacity of 11,100 units, that means the maximum production using maximum overtime would be 16,650 units (11,100 + 5,550).

You will incur overtime charges if you choose to produce more than your workers can manufacture given their current productivity levels. Your production employees are first assigned to produce the desired volume of Product 1. Once the appropriate number of workers have been assigned to Product 1 (based on their current productivity level for producing Product 1), the remaining workers are assigned to produce Product 2. If you have an insufficient number of workers to produce the total number of units you have entered when making your decisions, you will incur an overtime charge. Overtime charges are double the labor rate for each unit produced at overtime. The calculation of overtime charges is discussed in Chapter 5 – Making Decisions, under the heading Number of Units to Produce.

You can also choose to produce less than the total production capacity of your plant. While this decision increases the cost of making each unit because of fixed costs associated with owning your plant, your management team may decide it is in the best long-term interests of your company to produce below the plant's total possible manufacturing capacity. This is usually the consequence of the company having product inventory levels your team has determined to be excessive.

There is a regular turnover in your production work force as they quit to accept employment elsewhere. You will lose 10% of the workers you employ each quarter. This will occur after the current quarter's production operations have been completed but before the next quarter's operations begin. For example, if you started Quarter 2 with 35 workers, three would quit at the end of that quarter. Consequently, you would have 32 workers available to produce your products in Quarter 3. This means you will have a shrinking labor pool unless you hire workers to replace those that are lost to turnover.

There is also a 10% probability of losing one extra production worker to turnover each quarter. Because the low level of unemployment in the area provides many job opportunities, you will not be able to change the turnover conditions in your company.

Currently, you have only one source of supply for your raw plastic materials. This company has been a steady supplier. The owners have mandated that your management team deal exclusively with this supplier.

At present, the owners limit you to selling your product in one market area and in the current single geographical territory. How much you are able to sell in this territory will depend on how much effort you put into marketing your products compared to your competitors' efforts to sell their products. You must spend your money wisely and determine what mix of the marketing strategies will produce the best results.

Your team may borrow from the *Threshold* simulation bank for short-term periods in order to finance the normal operation of your business. After you have made your other decisions for a particular quarter, you can request a short-term loan to cover the cash shortages you expect. You can also borrow money from the *Threshold* bank to help finance an expansion of the production capacity of your manufacturing plant. You can borrow the money needed for this capital expenditure as a long-term mortgage.

YOUR COMPANY'S MARKETPLACE

Each company in the *Threshold* simulation sells the same two products. Initially, there is no difference in product quality between your products and your competitors' products. However, the investment your management team makes in product quality may create a differentiation in the consumer's mind. This will depend on what you spend improving product quality compared to what your competitors spend in this area. If you and your competitors all spend similar amounts, the customers may recognize that you have a high quality product, but see it as no different than your competitors' high quality product. In other words, how much you invest in quality on a relative basis is as important as how much you do on an absolute basis.

Fluctuations in the simulation's economic indicator, which gives some indication of the economy's health, can affect the demand for your products. A rising indicator signals a healthy economy. It indicates that business might be better than the market forecasts you can purchase from economic forecasters through the market research options on the Marketing and Market Research Decision screen. However, changes in the economy may not affect demand for all products equally. Your ability to analyze the market's reaction to your marketing efforts, and the efforts of your competitors, will affect your ability to market your products efficiently and effectively.

The customers in your company's marketplace, although value conscious, will not invest large amounts of time trying to find the company that offers the best value for its products. It may be tempting to pursue a strategy where you limit your company's marketing efforts, attempting to benefit from product awareness created by other companies' marketing efforts. However, potential customers may not recognize how good your product is if your promotional efforts lag too far behind your competitors'.

Advertising creates awareness of your product. Too little effort in this area and customers will not remember your brand name as they head out to make their purchase.

Further, if all companies adopt a low product promotion strategy, customers will stop buying this type of product at all and will begin buying substitute goods from companies outside your industry. Total industry demand will suffer. In the *Threshold* environment, a weak marketing effort may be doubly disastrous. Not only will one company suffer from a weak effort, but the whole industry may decline as well. All companies in the industry will then face an overcapacity problem (manufacturing capacity in excess of demand for the product) that in turn will create other problems.

The next two chapters will give detailed descriptions about how the *Threshold* simulation software works. They will also explain the marketing, production, and financial decisions you will have to make each quarter as you manage your business.

CHAPTER 4

USING THE COMPANY DISK

CHAPTER OVERVIEW

This chapter will introduce you to the computer and to the *Threshold* program on the company disk. It will explain how to:
- work with the *Threshold* program either with or without a mouse.
- make entries on the two decisions screens.
- move from one screen to another screen using (a) the PgDn and PgUp keys, (b) the Menu Bar displayed across the top of every screen, or (c) the *Threshold* "hot" keys.
- use the Menu Bar to perform various operations.

After reading this chapter, you should be familiar with the mechanics of working with *Threshold*. In the next chapter, we will discuss the decisions you will make to manage your *Threshold* company.

It is best to use the *Threshold* disk and the computer to try out each step as you read about it. Do not worry about entering decisions; any of the decisions you enter now you can change later. If you cannot get access to the computer as you read this chapter, you will still be able to understand the information presented here. Read the text and look at the sample screens in the text to see what you will see on the computer monitor. Then try everything out on a computer as soon as possible.

WHAT YOU NEED

The *Threshold* program has been designed to work on a personal computer with either an MS-DOS system or in the MS Windows environment (Windows 3.1x, Windows 95, and Windows NT). You can use these two systems interchangeably, DOS one time and Windows the next. Once you have loaded the program, all the commands for working with it are the same, regardless of whether you are using the DOS version or the Windows version. The only thing that is different is the command you use to load the version of *Threshold* you desire.

Computer System Requirements

Depending on which version of *Threshold* you plan to use, you will need to have access to a personal computer with the following characteristics.

MS-DOS Version. If you are using the DOS version of *Threshold*, your computer must have:
- 640K of memory (1 Meg is preferred).
- at least 1 disk drive.
- monochrome or color monitor.
- printer (optional).

MS Windows Version. If you are using the Windows version of *Threshold*, your computer must have:
- 4 Meg of memory with Windows 3.1 (8 Meg is preferred if using Windows 95 or Windows NT).
- 1 Meg of space on your hard disk.
- at least 1 disk drive.
- monochrome or color monitor.
- printer (optional).

Other Needs

You will also need:
- a *Threshold* company disk. This disk, also labeled as Setup Disk #2, is included with this manual.
- a blank disk suitable for use with the PC to use to make backup copies of your *Threshold* disk (strongly advised, but not required to operate *Threshold*).

NAVIGATING AROUND *THRESHOLD*

To work with *Threshold*, you need to be able to move within a screen and among the multiple screens that provide information on your *Threshold* company and its environment. What follows is a brief description of the methods you can use to do this. Specific directions for making entries and moving among *Threshold* screens is provided later in this chapter. If you are comfortable with navigating around *Threshold* after reading the following brief descriptions, you can choose to skip the detailed sections on "Moving Around" and "Moving From" the *Threshold* screens.

Using a Mouse vs. No Mouse

If you are familiar with working in a Windows environment, the *Threshold* program utilizes standard Windows protocol for key stroke entries. This means the Alt key highlights the Menu Bar options, the Tab key moves you to the next entry point, the Shift key + Tab key moves you backwards to the preceding entry point, and so forth. You can also use a mouse, if one is connected to your computer. Just as with Windows, you can use these two methods in combination with each other, switching back and forth as often as you like.

Using the PgUp and PgDn Keys.

You can use the Page Up and Page Down keys to move from one screen in the *Threshold* program to another. Pressing the PgUp or PgDn keys moves you to either the previous screen or the next screen, respectively.

Using "Hot" Keys.

The *Threshold* program also has a number of "hot" keys that let you to move from one screen to another screen. For example, pressing the CTRL key plus B moves you directly to the Balance Sheet report screen. Appendix F provides a listing of these special keys. These "hot" keys are also listed with their associated reports or screens when you access the options under the heading on the Menu bar. The Menu bar appears at the top of all screens when you are using the *Threshold* program.

THE COMPANY DISK

The company disk contains the *Threshold* computer program that gives instructions to your computer on how to run the simulation. As you enter your decisions on the screen, the *Threshold* program automatically stores them on your company disk. It is only necessary for you to enter your decisions on the two decisions screens (discussed below), and then to exit the program to have your decisions saved onto your disk.

We encourage you to make copies of your team's company disk. In fact, we strongly recommend that you make a backup copy of your disk after every time you make a new set of decisions or receive the results of your decision after your administrator has processed them. The information stored on your disk is important. You should keep a backup copy in case the original disk is lost, damaged, or destroyed. The process for making additional copies of your disk is described later in this chapter.

You may choose to make multiple copies of your team's company disk so that each member of your team can work with *Threshold* separately before team meetings. However, it is critical that you make all of your team's *final* decisions on the disk that you turn in to the administrator. When your team has made all of its management decisions for a quarter on your company disk, you will give this disk to the administrator.

The *final* set of numbers that you entered when making your decisions will be on your disk. Your administrator will use another *Threshold* program to read the decisions you and other teams have entered onto your respective team's disk. Once all of the team decisions have been read into the administrator's computer, the administrator will process those decisions to determine how each team performed in that particular quarter. The administrator will then store the results of that quarter on your disk and return it to your team. Once a quarter has been processed by your administrator, you cannot alter your decisions or the results for that quarter. Your next set of decisions will be for the next quarter of operation and will be based on the results of the quarter of operation you just completed. For example, once your administrator has processed the decisions for Quarter 2, your next set of decisions will be for Quarter 3 regardless of how much you would like to change what you did in Quarter 2. You cannot turn back the clock in the simulation anymore than you can in real life. When working with *Threshold*, once the administrator has processed your decisions, you must move forward – on to the next quarter of operation.

Having just said that you must always go forward to the next quarter when working with *Threshold*, your administrator may decide that special circumstances warrant re-processing a quarter. However, these situations are extremely rare, and will not occur just because you had a bad quarter of operation. Consequently, you should assume that once you have turned your decisions for a particular quarter into your administrator you will not be able to make changes to those decisions. Therefore, be certain the decisions you turn into your administrator are the ones with which you are willing to live. If your team has multiple backup copies of your disk, make sure that you turn in the disk with the decisions you want processed. *This is your responsibility, not the administrator's.* If you accidentally turn in the wrong disk you will have to live with the results of the decisions that were on that disk. Similarly, if you turn in the "right" disk, but with some experimental decisions on it, you will still be stuck with the results of those decisions. So be careful and manage your company disk prudently.

STARTING THE *THRESHOLD* PROGRAM

If you have access to a computer, you will want to try out each step discussed here, as you read about it. If not, read the instructions so you will be familiar with them when it is time to begin working with *Threshold*.

Start Your Computer

The first step in running *Threshold* is to start your computer. To do this, follow these steps:
1. Turn on the computer, monitor, and printer, if one is attached. If the computer is already on, press these three keys: [CTRL] [ALT] [DEL] (Control, Alt, and Delete keys) at the same time to restart the computer.

18   Chapter 4, Using the Company Disk

2. Wait while the computer performs several self-tests. If the computer was off, it may take 30 seconds for these self-tests to complete, so be patient. Depending on your computer's internal setup instructions and software, you will see either a C> prompt or Windows icons on the monitor.
3. If the computer you are using has a virus checking program on it, make sure the computer and your disk are free of any viruses. Not doing this could easily lead to a virus infecting not only your disk, but also any other computer with which your disk comes in contact.

Once your computer is operating and any virus checking programs on the computer are enabled, you will need to determine which version of *Threshold* you wish to use. As stated earlier, the *Threshold* program will work with either an MS-DOS system or in the MS Windows environment. Decide which version you are going to use and then go to the appropriate section. Remember, you can use these two systems interchangeably, DOS one time and Windows the next. Once you have loaded the program, all the commands for working with it are the same, regardless of whether you are using the DOS version or the Windows version. The only thing that is different is the command you use to load the version of *Threshold* you desire. We will discuss how to load the MS-DOS version of *Threshold* first.

Using the DOS Version of *Threshold*

1. Insert the company disk into the computer's disk drive with the label up. Usually this disk drive is designated in the computer's memory as Drive A. (If your computer is set up to read this disk drive as Drive B, substitute the letter B for the letter A in all instructions.)
2. If your monitor is displaying a C> prompt, switch to Drive A by typing **A:** and press [ENTER].

   Type **Thr** and press [ENTER] and wait while the computer loads the *Threshold* program. Depending on the speed of your computer, this may take from 15 to 30 seconds. You will see the opening *Threshold* screen. Press any key to begin the program and go to the chapter heading "The Initial Time You Start the *Threshold* Program" on the next page of this chapter.
3. If you are in a Windows environment you can still choose to use the DOS version. If you are in Windows 3.1x, click on the File menu of your Windows Program Manager and select the **Run** option. If you are in Windows 95 or Windows NT, click on the Start button and select the **Run** option. Insert the company disk in Drive A and type **a:thr** (or **b:thr** if your disk is in the Drive B) and click on OK. If you are using a network printer in a computer lab, you may have to exit to DOS to print using the DOS version of *Threshold*. Some networks do not allow the printing of DOS programs through a Windows environment. See the lab manager for help if you have questions.

Setting Up the Windows Version of *Threshold*

If this is the first time you are using the *Threshold* program on this computer, you must first run *Threshold's* setup program to ensure that certain Windows files needed to operate *Threshold* are in your Windows Systems directory. You will only need to run this setup program once, on each computer that you use. After that, just use the instructions under "Using the Windows Version of *Threshold*."

1. If you are in Windows (either 3.1x, 95, or NT), close any applications that are already open or that are opened as part of your Windows startup options. For example, if Microsoft Office automatically loads during your startup of Windows, you will need to close its applications. If you are in Windows 3.1x, do this by pressing [CTRL] + [ESC] to display the Task List dialogue box on your monitor. The only application you want open is Program Manager. Close all other applications by highlighting an application (e.g., Microsoft Office) and selecting the End Task

Chapter 4, Using the Company Disk   19

button. If you are in Windows 95 or Windows NT, do this by closing the applications that are open in the Task Bar displayed across the bottom of your monitor. Closing all applications will prevent any conflict that might arise between Windows files for *Threshold* that are being loaded and Windows Systems files that are currently in use.

2. If you are in Windows 3.1x, click on the File menu of your Windows Program Manager and select the **Run** option. If you are in Windows 95 or Windows NT, click on the Start button and select the **Run** option. Insert the *Threshold* Setup Disk #1 in Drive A and type **a:setup** (or **b:setup** if your disk is in the Drive B) and click on OK. Exhibit 4.1 will appear on your monitor to remind you to close all open applications. Select "Exit Setup" if you have any open applications, otherwise select OK.

Exhibit 4.1

![Threshold Company Setup dialog: Welcome to the Threshold Company installation program. Setup cannot install system files or update shared files if they are in use. Before proceeding, we recommend that you close any applications you may be running. Buttons: OK, Exit Setup.]

3. Wait while the files are loaded. You will be prompted to insert the second set up disk (also labeled as the *Threshold* Company disk) during this process. Next, Exhibit 4.2 will appear on your monitor. Unless you have a special need to change the directory where your *Threshold* company files will be stored, click on the button with the computer icon.

Exhibit 4.2

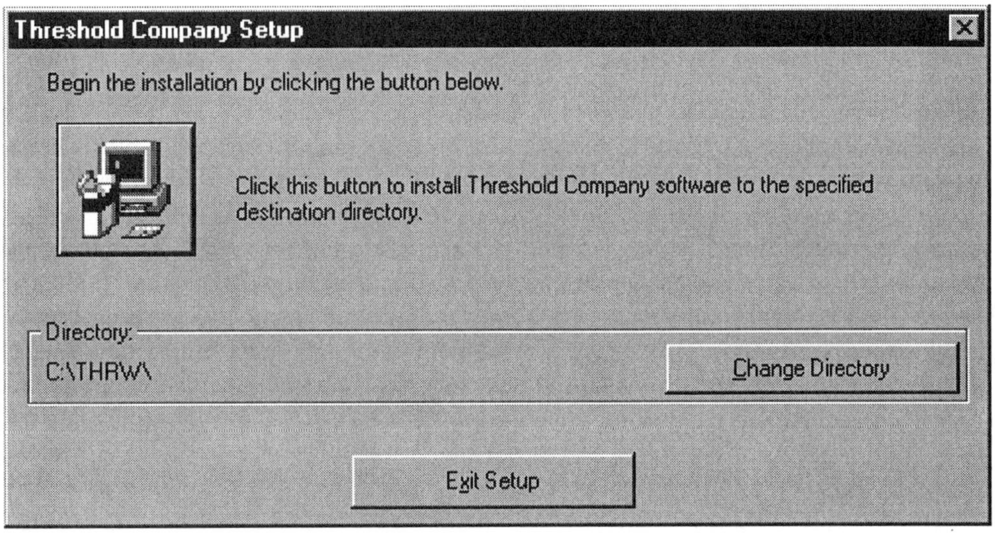

![Threshold Company Setup dialog: Begin the installation by clicking the button below. Click this button to install Threshold Company software to the specified destination directory. Directory: C:\THRW\. Buttons: Change Directory, Exit Setup.]

20   Chapter 4, Using the Company Disk

If you want to change where the files will be stored, select the "Change Directory" option and type in a name for the directory you want created to hold your *Threshold* company files. You must use DOS protocol for this entry. For example, if you want to store the files on your D hard drive and name the directory "thresh", type in **D:\thresh** and then select the computer icon. We recommend that you do not change the directory name and location unless absolutely necessary. After you have been prompted that the set up operation was successfully completed, go to the next section, "Using the Windows Version of *Threshold*".

Using the Windows Version of *Threshold*

1. If you are in Windows 3.1x, click on the File menu of your Windows Program Manager and select the **Run** option. If you are in Windows 95 or Windows NT, click on the Start button and select the **Run** option. Insert the company disk in Drive A and type **a:thrw** (or **b:thrw** if your disk is in the Drive B) and click on OK. Exhibit 4.3 shows an example of what this screen and your entry will look like. Remember, you need to have previously loaded *Threshold's* Windows files on this machine before you can successfully load the *Threshold* program. (If you want to use the *Threshold* icon to start the program, you will need to operate using the hard drive on the computer. Read the section on "Using a Hard Disk" on Page 36 to ensure you properly store your decision entries.)

2. Wait while the computer loads the *Threshold* program. Depending on the speed of your computer this may take 30 to 40 seconds. You will see the opening *Threshold* screen. Press any key to begin the program.

Exhibit 4.3

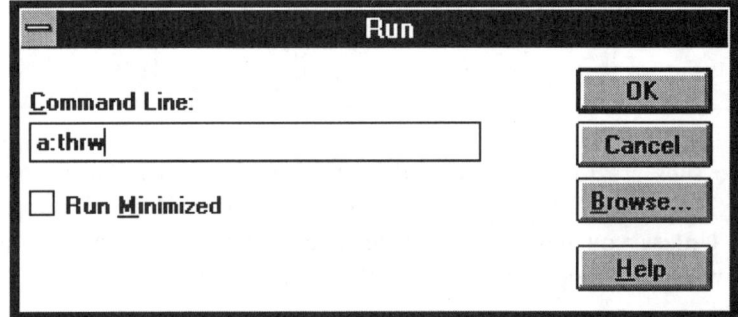

THE INITIAL TIME YOU START THE *THRESHOLD* PROGRAM

The first time you load the *Threshold* program, a screen will appear that will ask you to give your company a name (See Exhibit 4.4). It will also ask you to enter a password that will protect you from unwanted access to your company's files. Thereafter, you will be asked to enter this password when entering the *Threshold* program. If the correct password is not entered, the program will not proceed. If you desire, you can change your company's password and your company name later in the simulation exercise. Directions for changing either your company name or password are explained later in this chapter under Menu Bar Operations.

Exhibit 4.4

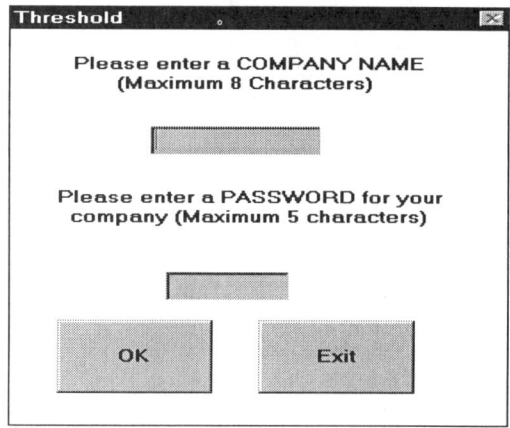

Entering a Company Name

Think of a name you would like to call your company. This name can be any combination of letters or numbers up to a maximum of eight (8) characters. There is no relationship between your company name and the success or failure of your company, so select any name that you desire. Type in this name and press the Tab key. This action will move the cursor to the cell for entering a password for your company disk.

Entering a Password

Think of a password for your company that you can easily remember. It is usually advisable not to select as a password the name of a family member or a nick-name that others are likely to guess. Your password can have a maximum of five (5) characters. Type in your password. Then press the Tab key until the OK button is highlighted and press [ENTER] or click on the OK button if you are using a mouse.

Make sure you protect your password and your company disk. If another team finds your company disk in a computer and knows your password, you give them access to all your company's records. You would no more want to do this than to give them printouts of your company reports.

THE *THRESHOLD* PROGRAM

Once you have loaded *Threshold*, seen the opening screen, pressed any key, and entered your password, you will see a screen that looks like Exhibit 4.5. (If you are working at the computer, this is what you should see now.)

Exhibit 4.5
Marketing & Market Research Decisions Screen

```
┌─────────────────────────────────────────────────────────────────────┐
│ UNKNOWN Industry    THRESHOLD Q 1 FORECAST      DEMO Company  0     │
│ File  Decision  Reports  Info  Print                                │
│                                                                     │
│                   ENTER MARKETING DECISIONS                         │
│                                                                     │
│                                     Product 1    Product 2          │
│                                                                     │
│         Price              ($)         64           47              │
│         TV Ads          (Minutes)       6            5              │
│         Newspaper (Column Inches)       9            7              │
│         Magazine Ads    (Pages)         8            7              │
│                                                                     │
│         Sales Forecast  (Units)       6000         5100             │
│                                                                     │
│                                                                     │
│                ENTER MARKETING RESEARCH DECISIONS                   │
│                                                                     │
│     Price              N      Product Quality              N        │
│     TV Ads             N      Units Sold                   N        │
│     Newspaper Ads      N      Future Sales Potential (Qtr) 1        │
│     Magazine Ads       N                                            │
│                                                                     │
└─────────────────────────────────────────────────────────────────────┘
```

This is the first of two screens on which your team will enter its decisions for Quarter 1, and for subsequent quarters as you move through the simulation exercise. What follows is a preview of *Threshold* that describes how to enter decisions, move around a decision screen, and move from one screen to another screen. You may choose to skip these sections and go to the "Menu Bar Operations" section if you are familiar with working in a Windows environment.

Threshold has two screens where you will enter your decisions regarding the operation of your business. These are the Marketing & Market Research Decisions screen (See Exhibit 4.5) and the Production & Finance Decisions screen (See Exhibit 4.6). In addition to these two screens, there are a number of screens that will display reports showing the results of the decisions you made. The two decisions screens will have a flashing cursor to guide you in entering your decisions. You cannot make entries on any of the report screens. Consequently, there is no need to move the cursor around those screens and no cursor will appear when you are viewing a report screen.

ENTERING A DECISION

The *Threshold* program will only allow you to make certain entries in specific locations. This is to prevent you from making entry mistakes. If you attempt an invalid entry (e.g., a number that is too large for the decision being made or a letter where a number is required), the *Threshold* program will indicate this by displaying an error message on the screen. You can access information on acceptable limits for your *Threshold* decisions through the Info heading on the Menu Bar, or by using certain *Threshold* "hot" keys. Just how to access this information on your company disk will be explained later in this chapter. You can also find the acceptable limits for *Threshold's* decisions in Appendix E of this manual.

SAVING YOUR DECISIONS

The *Threshold* program automatically saves any entries you make whenever you exit the *Threshold* program. This means the only way you will not save the entries you make onto your company disk is if you either shut off the computer or remove the disk before exiting the program. As will be explained later, you can always change any entries you have made and saved onto your disk up to the time you hand in your disk to your administrator for processing. Once your decisions for a quarter have been processed you can no longer change them.

CORRECTING AN ERROR

If you make a mistake or want to change something you have typed, simply move to the number you want to change using either the Tab key or the mouse. Type in your new decision and press the Tab key. This will replace the old number with your new number.

MOVING THE CURSOR AROUND *THRESHOLD'S* DECISION SCREENS

You can move the cursor around the two decisions screens by either of two methods. One method is to use the Tab key. The second method is to use the mouse, if one is connected to your computer. You can use each of these methods in combination with the other method. This means you can make one move using the mouse and the next move using the Tab key. You can switch back and forth between these two methods of moving around a decisions screen as often as you like. Each of the two methods is described briefly, below.

Using the Tab Key

When the decisions screen first appears, a flashing cursor will appear next to the first decision you must make – the price of Product 1. Use the Tab key to move from decision to decision on the screen. Pressing the Tab key alone will move you "forward" to the next decision entry cell. Pressing and holding the Shift key and then pressing the Tab key will move you "backward" to the preceding decision entry cell. When you reach the "last" decision on the screen, pressing the Tab key will take you back to the "first" decision on the screen. You can enter the individual decisions in any order you choose. What matters is the last set of numbers showing on the screen after you have finished entering decisions.

If you do not want to change the number shown on the screen, press the Tab key to move to the next decision you must make. This will automatically enter the number displayed on the screen. If you wish to make a change, simply type in your new number (or letter) and press the Tab key. This will enter your new number (or letter) and move you to the next decision. Notice that when you tab to a new cell, the whole cell is highlighted. If you press the Backspace key, the whole number is erased. You must then enter a new number and press the Tab key or the *Threshold* program will automatically enter a zero for that decision.

If you press an Arrow key while the number is highlighted, the highlighting will disappear, but the number will remain. You can then use the Arrow key to move to a digit within the number and make a change to the existing number without having to change the whole number. For example, you could change a sales forecast number from 6,100 to 6,150. To *insert* a digit into an existing number, use the Arrow key to move to the insertion point, type in the new digit, use the Delete or the Backspace key to remove any unwanted digit(s), and press the Tab key. To *type over* a particular digit, use the Arrow key to move to the digit you want to replace, press the Insert key, then type in the new digit and tab to the next decision cell. Notice how the shape of the flashing cursor changes after you press the Insert key. Once you have pressed the Insert key, you will be able to type over existing numbers until you press the Insert key again and the flashing cursor returns to its original shape.

Using the Mouse

Use the mouse to move around a decision screen the same as you would when working in a Windows environment. Simply move the mouse indicator to the decision number you want to change and click the left mouse button. The number you selected will become highlighted. Type in the number you desire and either press the Tab key or click onto a new number. Repeat this process until you have made all the changes you desire to the decisions showing on the screen.

Clicking twice on a number will allow you to edit the existing number on the screen. The first click highlights the number. The second click positions the cursor in the number so that you can type in a digit and delete unwanted digits using the Backspace or Delete keys. As with working without a mouse, pressing the Insert key allows you to type over existing numbers.

You will need to enter information on only two screens -- the two decisions screens. If you are at the computer, try entering some information on the Marketing & Market Research Decisions screen now. None of the numbers you enter at this time will become permanent. Even during the simulation exercise, no decision is permanent until your administrator processes the quarter's decisions. This means the only numbers that matter are the *last* ones you enter onto your disk before handing it in to your administrator. So feel free to experiment now. Chapter 5 explains each of the decisions you will enter on the two decisions screens regarding Marketing, Production, and Finance.

MOVING FROM SCREEN TO SCREEN

Threshold has a number of screens that you can view and/or print out when working on the exercise. These are: (a) the decisions screens, on which you enter your decisions, (b) the reports screens, where you can see the results of decisions you have made, and (c) the information screens, which provide you with information on various parts of *Threshold*, such as the costs of your operations. There are three methods that you can use for moving from screen to screen. One method is to use a combination of the PgUp and PgDn keys as described earlier. The second method is to use the Menu Bar displayed across the top of the *Threshold* screen. The third method is to use *Threshold's* "hot" keys to move directly to a decision, report, or information screen. We will now discuss each of the three methods, in turn.

Using the PgUp and PgDn Keys

To move from screen to screen using the PgUp and PgDn keys, press:
- [PgUp]   to move back to the previous screen.
- [PgDn]   to move to the next screen.

Press [PgDn] to see the next screen. You should now see the second decisions screen, the Production & Finance Decisions Screen (Exhibit 4.6).

Exhibit 4.6
Production & Finance Decisions Screen

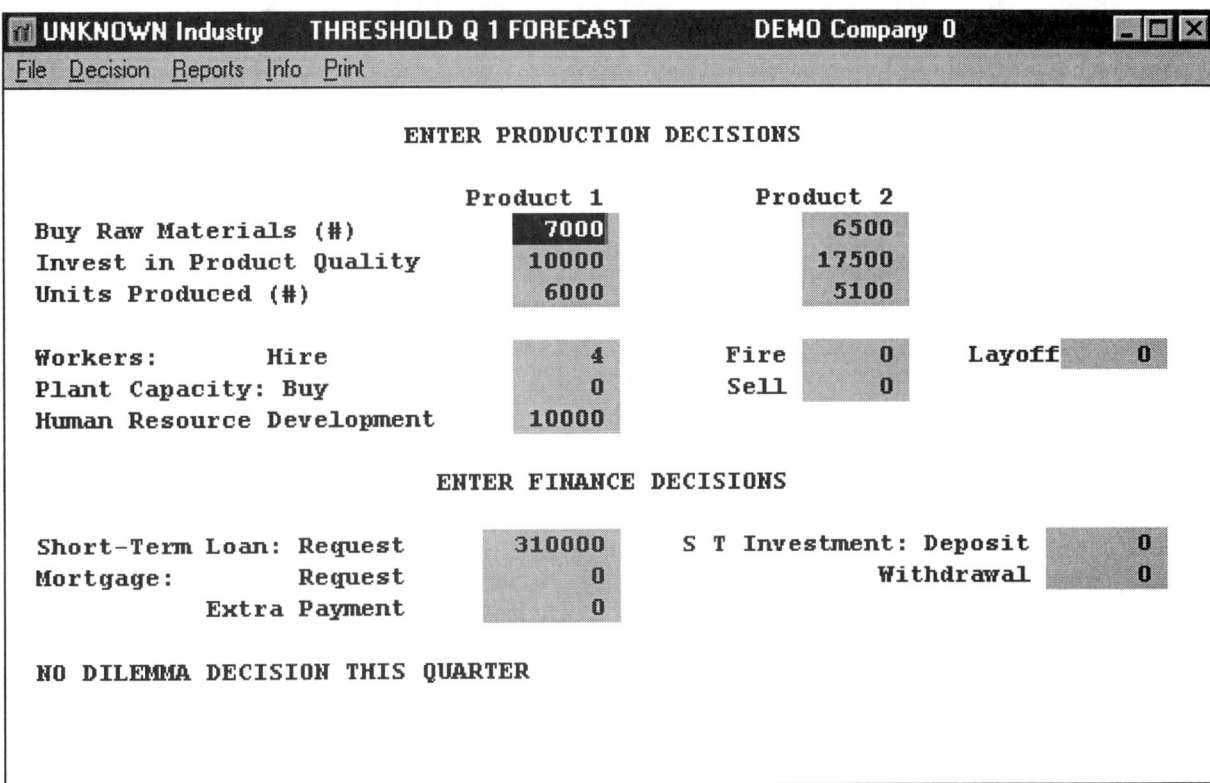

The Report Screens. Press [PgDn] again. This time you will see the first of the report screens, the Inventory report (See Exhibit 4.7). We will explain this and the other report screens later, in Chapter 6. Continue pressing [PgDn] to see the rest of the reports. The sequence in which the report screens appear is as follows:
- Inventory Report
- Labor Report
- Cost of Production Report
- Selling and Administrative Costs Report
- Income Statement
- Balance Sheet
- Cash Flow Statement
- Market Research Report
- Quarter Performance Report
- Game-to-Date Performance Report
- Cost Parameters Report
- Marketing & Finance Limits and Time Lags Report
- Production Limits and Time Lags Report
- Bulletin

Exhibit 4.7

```
┌─────────────────────────────────────────────────────────────────────────┐
│  UNKNOWN Industry    THRESHOLD Q 1 FORECAST         DEMO Company 0      │
│ File  Decision  Reports  Info  Print                                    │
├─────────────────────────────────────────────────────────────────────────┤
│                                                                         │
│   Raw Material Inventory         Product 1            Product 2         │
│                              Units      Value      Units     Value      │
│                                                                         │
│   Beginning Balance           500        4000        400      4800      │
│   Units Received             7000       56000       6500     78000      │
│   Total Available            7500       60000       6900     82800      │
│   Used in Production         6000       48000       5100     61200      │
│   Ending Balance             1500       12000       1800     21600      │
│   Raw Matl Warehouse Costs    500         500        400       800      │
│   Total Product Cost                    48500                62000      │
│                                                                         │
│   Finished Good Inv.             Product 1            Product 2         │
│                              Units  $/Unit  Value  Units  $/Unit  Value │
│                                                                         │
│   Beginning Balance             0    .00      0      0    .00      0   │
│   Production                 6000  37.50 225026   5100  40.38 205954   │
│   Units to Sell              6000  37.50 225026   5100  40.38 205954   │
│   Units Sold                 6000  37.50 225026   5100  40.38 205954   │
│   End Balance                   0    .00      0      0    .00      0   │
│   FG Warehouse                  0   2.50      0      0   1.50      0   │
│   Lost Sales                    0  64.00      0      0  47.00      0   │
│                                                                         │
└─────────────────────────────────────────────────────────────────────────┘
```

If you are working on the computer, try pressing [PgDn] and [PgUp] a number of times each until you are familiar with their operation.

Using the Menu Bar

You can also access each of the reports/screens listed above through the Menu Bar. The Menu Bar is always shown across the top of your screen, regardless of what particular screen you are viewing. There are five headings listed on the Menu Bar File, Decision, Reports, Info, and Print. Under each of these headings are a number of options that you can use. For example, as shown in Exhibit 4.8, under the File heading you have the option to (a) Select Quarter, (b) Change Password, (c) Change Company Name, and (d) Exit.

Exhibit 4.8

```
┌─────────────────────────────────────────────────────────────────────┐
│ ─  UNKNOWN Industry      THRESHOLD Q 1 FORECAST      DEMO Company 0  ▼▲│
├─────────────────────────────────────────────────────────────────────┤
│ File  Decision  Reports  Info  Print                                 │
│ ┌─────────────────────────┐                                          │
│ │ Select Quarter          │         MARKETING                        │
│ │ Change Password         │                                          │
│ │ Change Company Name     │            Product 1    Product 2        │
│ ├─────────────────────────┤                                          │
│ │ Exit                    │                                          │
│ └─────────────────────────┘                                          │
│          Price              ($)          64           47             │
│          TV Ads             (Minutes)     6            5             │
│          Newspaper (Column Inches)        9            7             │
│          Magazine Ads       (Pages)       8            7             │
│                                                                      │
│          Sales Forecast     (Units)     6000         5100            │
│                                                                      │
│                           MARKETING RESEARCH                         │
│                                                                      │
│     Price                    N      Product Quality              N   │
│     TV Ads                   N      Units Sold                   N   │
│     Newspaper Ads            N      Future Sales Potential (Qtr) 1   │
│     Magazine Ads             N                                       │
│                                                                      │
└─────────────────────────────────────────────────────────────────────┘
```

There are two methods you can use to access each of the headings on the Menu Bar and the options associated with each heading. One method is to use a mouse, the other is to use a combination of the ALT and Arrow keys. As with the decisions screens, you can use each of these methods in combination with the other method. We describe both methods for accessing the Menu Bar below.

Using the Mouse. To access a heading on the Menu Bar using the mouse, simply click on the heading with which you want to work. The options available for that heading are automatically displayed. To select an option, just click on it with the mouse.

Using the ALT and Arrow Keys. To access the Menu Bar, press the ALT key. Notice that the heading labeled as "File" becomes highlighted. Notice also that the first letter in each of the other headings is either highlighted or underlined, depending on whether you are using the DOS or Windows version of *Threshold*, respectively. Pressing the → and ← arrow keys will move you to the other headings on the Menu Bar. You can also move directly to a heading by pressing the letter that is either highlighted or underlined for each option.

To access the options under each heading, press the ↓ (i.e., down) arrow key. A list of options available under that heading will appear on your screen. To select one of those options, press the down arrow key until your desired option is highlighted and press [ENTER]. Alternatively, each one of the options will have a letter that is highlighted or underlined. Pressing that letter on your keyboard will also serve to select that option. Each of the options available through the Menu Bar headings will be discussed later in this chapter. For now, concentrate on the mechanics of moving from screen to screen using the Menu Bar.

Notice that once the options for a particular heading have been displayed, pressing an arrow key to move to the next heading will automatically display the options for that heading. The options for the headings will continue to remain displayed until you press either the ALT key again or the ESC key.

Using *Threshold's* "Hot" Keys

In addition to using a combination of the ALT and Arrow keys or the mouse, you can also directly access certain screens using *Threshold's* "hot" keys. These "hot" keys are shown after each option and are also listed in Appendix F. For example, when you access the Reports menu options, you will see that you can access each of the options directly using the CTRL key, plus a letter or a function key. To use the "hot" keys, press and hold the CTRL key, then press the appropriate letter or function key. For example, if you press and hold the CTRL key and press C, the Cash Flow Statement will appear on the screen.

You can access screens using the "hot" keys regardless of where you are in the *Threshold* program. This means you do not have to be using the Reports Menu to access a report using a "hot" key. For example, if you are viewing a decisions screen (e.g., the Marketing & Market Research screen) and press and hold the CTRL key and then press C, you will move directly to the Cash Flow Statement screen. However, if you have pressed the ALT key and highlighted the Menu Bar, the "hot" keys are disabled. They will not work while you are accessing the Menu Bar options. Pressing [ESC] will take you out of the Menu Bar and enable the "hot" keys for your use. Learning to use *Threshold*'s "hot" keys allows you to move quickly around the program and can shorten the time necessary to make a decision.

You now should know how to move around the decisions screens and to move from one screen to another. Next we will describe what each of the options under the Menu Bar headings can do.

MENU BAR OPERATIONS

The Menu Bar contains five headings: File, Decision, Reports, Info, and Print. Using the Menu Bar will allow you to work with the *Threshold* files on your company disk, enter decisions for managing your company, view reports on your company's operation, access information regarding *Threshold*, and print out any, or all, of the screens you can view. Each of these is discussed below.

The File Menu

You can perform four different operations using the File menu (See Exhibit 4.8). These are: Select Quarter, Change Password, Change Company Name, and Exit. Each of these will be discussed in order.

Select Quarter. The Select Quarter option allows you to change from the current quarter in which you are operating and select an earlier quarter of company operations. This will allow you to access earlier company reports and to view or print out that information. The *Threshold* program retains all of your company's history on your company's disk. You will have the ability to view, and print, any or all of your company's reports, etc., from Quarter 0 through the current quarter of operation. However, this option will not allow you to return to an earlier quarter and change the decisions that you made back then. Time marches forward, not backward.

To select a particular quarter, choose the Select Quarter option. Exhibit 4.9 shows the screen that will appear on your monitor. Enter the number of the quarter desired and select OK. If you select a quarter that has already been processed, the two decisions screens will not be displayed. If you select a quarter beyond the current quarter (e.g., Quarter 3 when you are making decisions for Quarter 2), you will receive an error message on the screen.

Exhibit 4.9

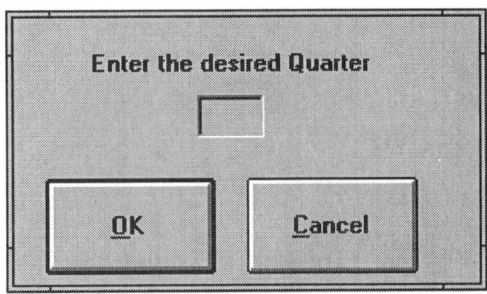

Take note: You will need to use this option to view and/or print the results of a quarter that has just been processed. After a quarter has been processed, the *Threshold* program will automatically load your company files for the next quarter of operation rather than the quarter that has just been processed. This means after Quarter 2 has been processed, Quarter 3 will appear on the screen when you load the *Threshold* program. To see the results of your Quarter 2 decisions and any market research information you have purchased, you will have to choose the Select Quarter option and enter a 2 as the desired quarter number. You can then choose to view or print these results. Once you are ready to begin entering Quarter 3 decisions, choose the Select Quarter option again and enter a 3 as the quarter number.

You may wonder why the *Threshold* program does not automatically load up the quarter that was just processed so that you could easily see the results of your decisions. We made this programming decision because most times when you load *Threshold* it will be to enter decisions for the next quarter. After reviewing and printing the results of last quarter's decisions, you will typically want to go straight to the next quarter's decision screens when loading *Threshold*.

Change Password. The first time you entered the *Threshold* program, you gave your company disk a password to prevent unwanted access to your company's reports that are stored on your disk. You may decide, for security reasons, to change your disk's password. This option allows you to make that change. You can change your password as often as you wish, but be careful. Frequent changes can lead to confusion about what is your password. If this happens, you will not be able to access the files on your disk, nor to make decisions for the upcoming quarter of operation. If this happens, see your administrator for help.

To change your password, select the Change Password option. Exhibit 4.10 shows the screen that will appear on your monitor. Enter a new password you will remember and press [ENTER] or click on OK. Again, it is usually advisable not to select as a password the name of a family member or a nickname that others are likely to guess.

Exhibit 4.10

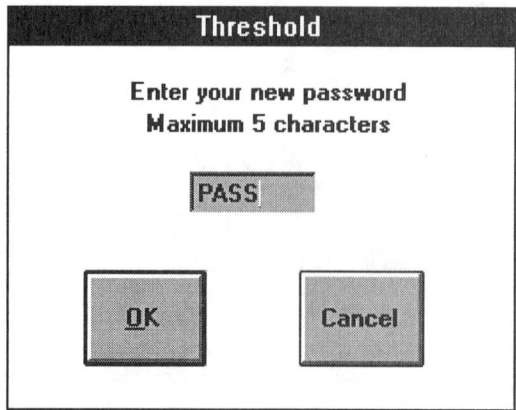

Change Company Name. As with the password, the first time you entered the *Threshold* program, you also gave your company a name that was saved onto your disk. As stated earlier, there is no relationship between your company name and the success or failure of your company. However, if you wish to change your company name at any time during the simulation exercise, you may use this option to do so.

To change your company name, select the Change Company Name option. Exhibit 4.11 shows the screen that will appear on your monitor. Type in your new company name and press [ENTER] or click on OK.

Exhibit 4.11

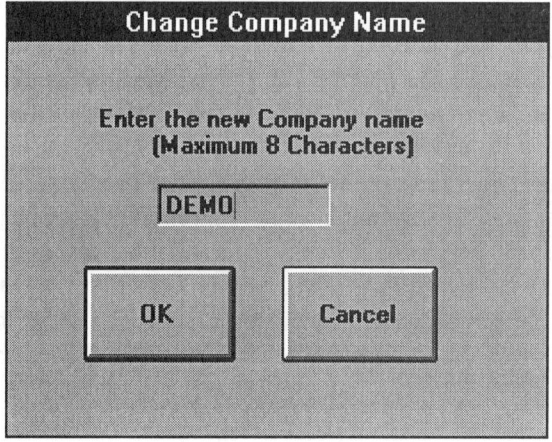

Exit. Selecting this option will take you out of the *Threshold* program and return you to the DOS prompt or to Windows. To do this, simply select the Exit option and press [ENTER]. You can also exit the program by selecting the File heading and then pressing X. Whenever you exit the *Threshold* program, the last numbers that were on the screens will be saved automatically on to your company disk.

The Decision Menu

The Decision menu option provides you with access to the two screens where you will enter your decisions for managing your company's operations (See Exhibit 4.12). Each of these will be discussed in order. Remember, you can access the decisions screens using either the Menu Bar or *Threshold*'s "hot" keys. Press the F1 Function key to move to the Marketing & Market Research Decisions Screen. Press F2 to move to the Production & Finance Decisions Screen.

Exhibit 4.12

```
┌─────────────────────────────────────────────────────────────────────────┐
│ —  UNKNOWN Industry    THRESHOLD Q 1 FORECAST      DEMO Company 0  ▼▲  │
│ File  Decision  Reports  Info  Print                                    │
│       ┌──────────────────────────────────┐                              │
│       │ Marketing and Market Research F1 │                              │
│       │ Production and Finance        F2 │ ETING                        │
│       └──────────────────────────────────┘                              │
│                                        Product 1     Product 2          │
│                                                                         │
│            Price              ($)         64            47              │
│            TV Ads        (Minutes)         6             5              │
│            Newspaper (Column Inches)       9             7              │
│            Magazine Ads     (Pages)        8             7              │
│                                                                         │
│            Sales Forecast   (Units)      6000          5100             │
│                                                                         │
│                          MARKETING RESEARCH                             │
│                                                                         │
│       Price              N      Product Quality              N          │
│       TV Ads             N      Units Sold                   N          │
│       Newspaper Ads      N      Future Sales Potential (Qtr) 1          │
│       Magazine Ads       N                                              │
│                                                                         │
└─────────────────────────────────────────────────────────────────────────┘
```

Marketing & Market Research. This screen allows you to enter your decisions regarding pricing, advertising, and quality for the two products your company is marketing. It also allows you to purchase market research about your competitors' marketing activities and the forecasted industry-wide demand for each of the products in future quarters. You will also use this screen to enter your forecasts for the sales volume you expect to achieve for each of your two products for the current quarter of operation.

To access this screen using the Menu Bar, select the Marketing & Market Research option and press [ENTER]. For directions on making entries on this screen, refer to the section "Moving Around *Threshold*'s Two Decisions Screens" at the beginning of this chapter.

Production & Finance. This screen allows you to enter your decisions regarding the production of your two products. This involves the ordering of raw materials, staffing and training of workers, setting production volumes, investing in the quality of your product and in the development of your production workers, and adjusting plant capacity to meet production needs. It also allows you to arrange the financing of your marketing and production activities. In some quarters of operation, you may be confronted with a management dilemma that will require a decision from you. On those occasions, you will enter that decision on this screen.

The Reports Menu

The Reports menu allows you to access the reports detailing your company's operation. Exhibit 4.13 shows the reports that you can view using this option. When accessing these reports, *Threshold* will always display the reports for the most current quarter of operation. If you want to view an earlier quarter, you must first use the Select Quarter option under the File menu heading, as was discussed above. A discussion of each of the reports available in *Threshold* is provided in Chapter 6.

Exhibit 4.13

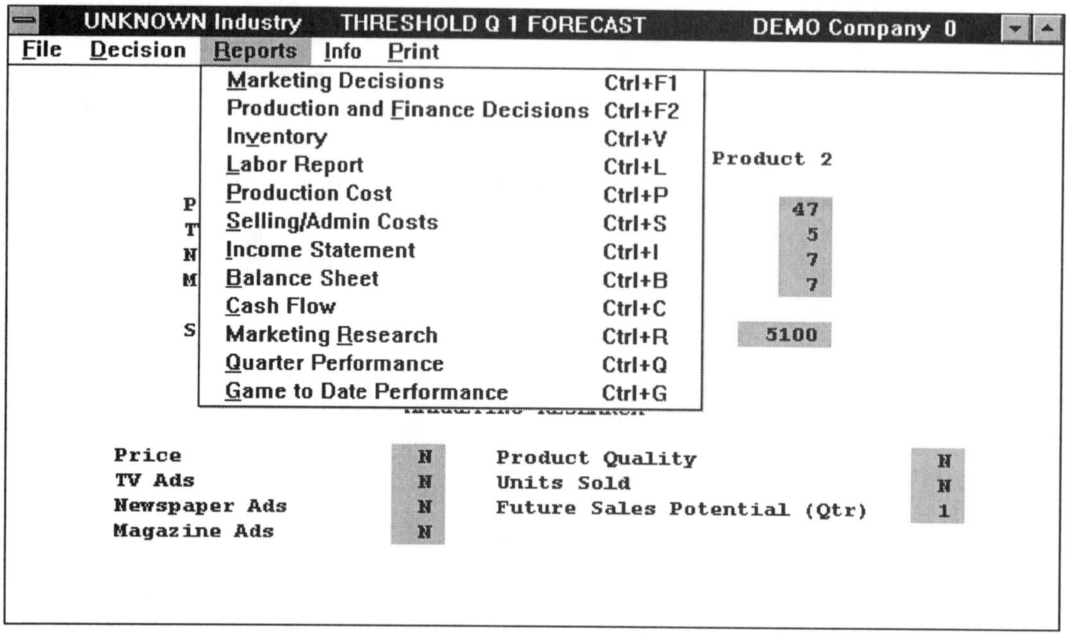

```
 UNKNOWN Industry    THRESHOLD Q 1 FORECAST         DEMO Company 0
File  Decision  Reports  Info  Print
                 Marketing Decisions              Ctrl+F1
                 Production and Finance Decisions Ctrl+F2
                 Inventory                        Ctrl+V
                 Labor Report                     Ctrl+L   Product 2
            P    Production Cost                  Ctrl+P
            T    Selling/Admin Costs              Ctrl+S      47
            N    Income Statement                 Ctrl+I       5
            M    Balance Sheet                    Ctrl+B       7
                 Cash Flow                        Ctrl+C       7
            S    Marketing Research               Ctrl+R    5100
                 Quarter Performance              Ctrl+Q
                 Game to Date Performance         Ctrl+G

            Price                N       Product Quality              N
            TV Ads               N       Units Sold                   N
            Newspaper Ads        N       Future Sales Potential (Qtr) 1
            Magazine Ads         N
```

The Info Menu

The Info menu provides you with access to the decision entry limits and costs involved in managing your *Threshold* company (See Exhibit 4.14). You can also access the Bulletin through the Info heading. We will discuss each of these options below.

Exhibit 4.14

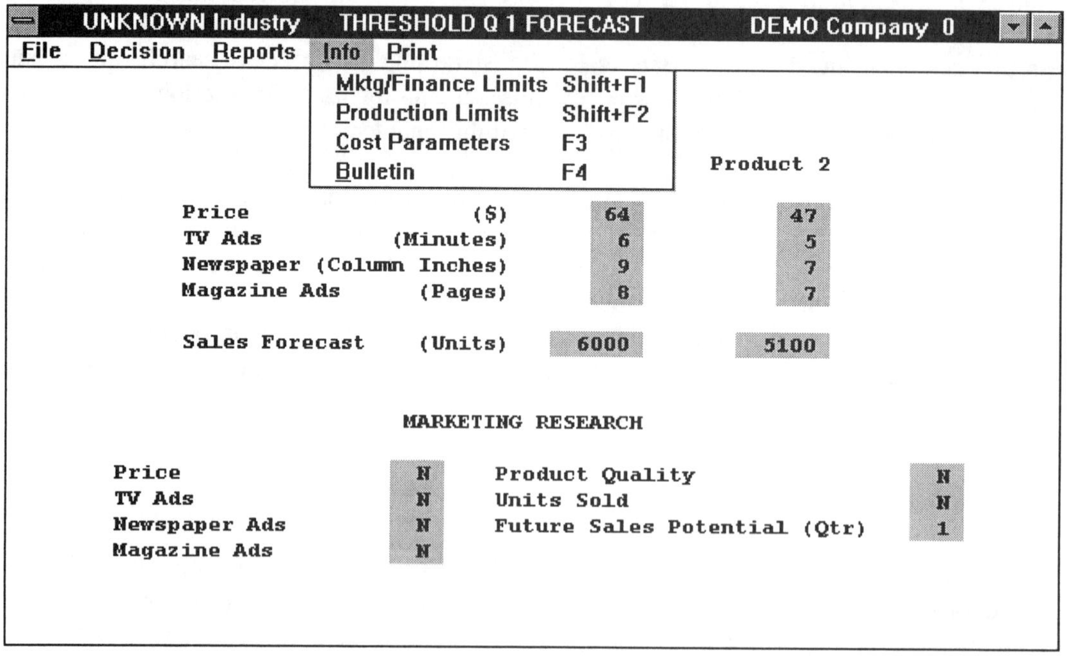

```
 UNKNOWN Industry    THRESHOLD Q 1 FORECAST         DEMO Company 0
File  Decision  Reports  Info  Print
                    Mktg/Finance Limits  Shift+F1
                    Production Limits    Shift+F2
                    Cost Parameters      F3
                    Bulletin             F4          Product 2

       Price                    ($)            64         47
       TV Ads                   (Minutes)       6          5
       Newspaper (Column Inches)               9          7
       Magazine Ads             (Pages)         8          7

       Sales Forecast           (Units)       6000       5100

                      MARKETING RESEARCH

       Price                 N       Product Quality              N
       TV Ads                N       Units Sold                   N
       Newspaper Ads         N       Future Sales Potential (Qtr) 1
       Magazine Ads          N
```

Marketing and Finance Limits Report. Accessing this option will display the acceptable limits for decision entries relating to marketing and finance. These include limits such as price ranges and maximum advertising levels. The screen also shows whether the decision will take effect in the current quarter (i.e., immediately) or in the following quarter (i.e., a one-quarter lag). You can also access the Marketing and Finance Limits screen using a "hot" key by pressing and holding the Shift key and then pressing F1.

Production Limits Report. Accessing this option will display the acceptable limits for decision entries relating to production. These include, for example, limits on Human Resource expenditures and the purchase of raw materials. As with the Marketing and Finance Limits Screen, it also shows whether the decision will take effect in the current quarter (i.e., immediately) or in the following quarter (i.e., one-quarter lag). You can also access the Production Limits Screen using a "hot" key by pressing and holding the Shift key and then pressing F2.

Cost Parameters Report. Selecting this option will provide you with a listing of the costs for various items associated with operating your *Threshold* company. These include, for example, the costs for advertising, workers' wages and productivity levels, inventory storage, and interest rates. You can also access the Cost Parameters Screen using a "hot" key by pressing the F3 function key.

Bulletin. The Bulletin gives you notices of pending changes or general information that your administrator wants to pass on to you. This information can, and most likely will, change every quarter. Do not forget to check it for new messages after your administrator has processed a quarter's decisions. It is your responsibility to be aware of the information provided in the Bulletin. You can also access the Bulletin screen using the F4 "hot" key.

The Print Menu

The Print menu allows you to print any screen that appears on your monitor. You can choose to print an individual screen, a selection of screens, or all screens, using this menu (See Exhibit 4.15). You can use this menu to print the screens you have selected to a printer connected to your computer, or to create a file for transferring the file electronically to a distant location using a modem.

Exhibit 4.15

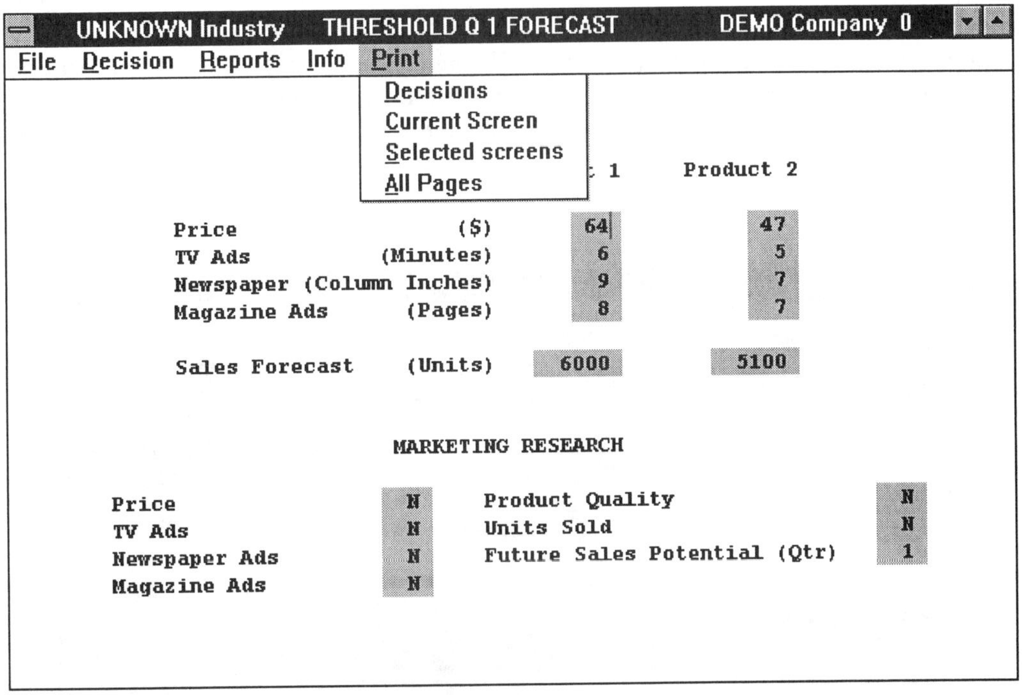

34   Chapter 4, Using the Company Disk

Decisions. Selecting this option will print the two decisions screens: Marketing & Market Research and Production & Finance. To print these two screens, select the Print heading using the mouse or the Tab key, then select the Decisions option.

A print dialogue screen will appear on your monitor so you can decide where you want to print the two screens (See Exhibit 4.16). If you want to send the screens to the printer connected to your computer, use the Tab key to move to the OK button and then press [ENTER] or use the mouse select the OK button.

Exhibit 4.16

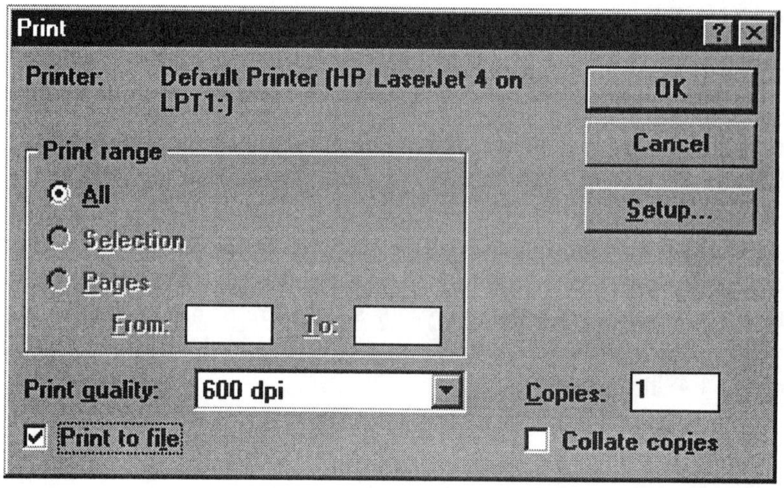

You also have the option of printing to a file instead of a printer. You could then transfer the file electronically to a teammate at another location using a modem. If you want to select this option, use the Tab key to move the cursor to the "Print to File" option in the lower left corner of the dialogue box, then press the space bar to "check" (✓) the box. Alternatively, you can use the mouse to check the box. Then select the OK button.

Another dialogue box will appear on your monitor prompting you to name the file and select the location where you want to save the file (See Exhibit 4.17). A default file name will appear in the upper left corner. If you wish to change the file name, select a file name that describes the contents of the file. File names can be up to eight characters long. To store that file on your company disk located in Drive A, select the "**a:**" drive option and press the Tab key to move to the OK button or use the mouse to click on OK.

Exhibit 4.17

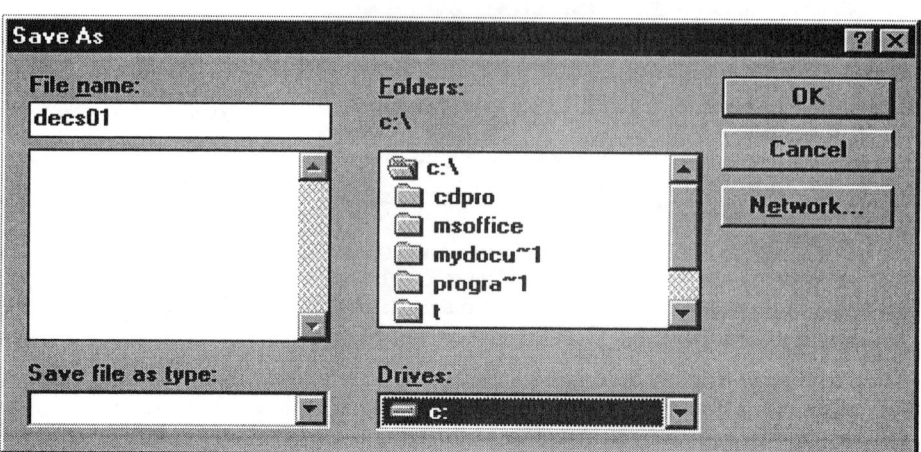

Current Screen. This option lets you print out the last screen you were viewing before selecting this option. As with the Print Decisions option, a print dialogue screen will appear on your monitor so you can decide where you want to print the two screens (See Exhibit 4.16). Select the OK button to print the screen. To save the screen as a file, check (✓) the Print to File option box, then select the OK button.

Selected Screens. This option allows you to print only the report screens you desire. After selecting this option, a screen will appear with a listing of the reports you can choose to print (See Exhibit 4.18). Use the mouse to click on the report(s) you desire (e.g., the Income Statement) or use the Tab key to move to the screen you want printed and then press the space bar to select that screen. When you have selected all the screens desired, use the Tab key to move to the OK button and press [ENTER] or click on OK using the mouse.

Exhibit 4.18

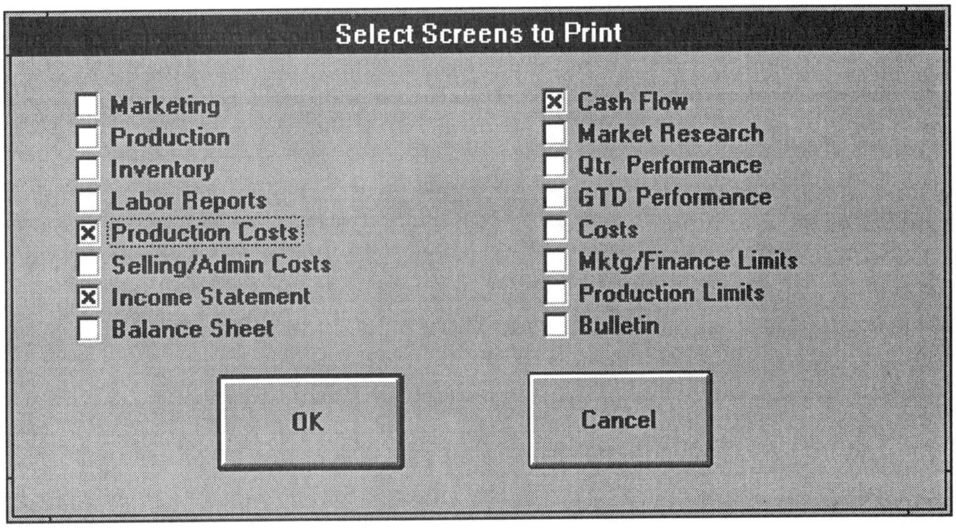

All Pages. This option will automatically print all of the *Threshold* screens. As with the Print Decisions option, a print dialogue screen will appear on your monitor so you can decide where you want to print the two screens (See Exhibit 4.16). Select the OK button to print the screen. To save the screen as a file, check (✓) the Print to File option box, then select the OK button.

SEEING THE *FORECASTED* RESULTS OF YOUR DECISIONS

Once you have entered decisions, you can view the *forecasted* reports for your company. These are not your "actual" results, like those that will be on your disk after the administrator has processed your decisions. Instead, these reports are based on the sales forecast that you entered on the Marketing & Market Research decisions screen. So, if you said, for example, that you will sell 6,000 units of Product 1 at a price of $40, you will see in the reports that you sold 6,000 units and made $240,000 in sales. However, when the *Threshold* program processes your decisions, your sales may look very different! For example, if you only sell 5,000 units because of aggressive pricing by your competitors, your sales revenues for Product 1 would only be $200,000. This reduction in sales revenues could move you from a profit to a loss for that quarter's operation. In other words, your forecast reports are only as accurate as your sales forecasts. If you are overly optimistic in your sales forecasts, your reports will reflect this optimism and may show profits that will be non-existent after your administrator processes all of the companies' decisions. The program will not warn you that your forecasts are inaccurate. It will only process your forecasts, not judge them. It is up to you to enter realistic decisions. Chapter 5 discusses making a sales forecast in more detail.

You can view the reports to see what will be the effects of your decisions, *assuming that your forecast is correct*. You can look through the reports using any one of the three methods for moving around the screens described above. Notice that before your administrator processes your decisions, the reports are labeled as "Forecast" reports. After the administrator has processed all the company disks the reports will be labeled as "Actual" reports. The "Actual" reports are the ones that matter. These are the reports that will be used to determine your standing relative to your competition and that you will use to determine your decisions for your company's next quarter of operation.

SEEING THE <u>*ACTUAL*</u> RESULTS OF EARLIER QUARTERS

As discussed above, when you load the *Threshold* program, it automatically advances to the next quarter for which you must make decisions. This means that if you want to view or print the actual results for earlier quarters of your company's operations (e.g., the quarter just processed by your administrator), you will have to use the Select Quarter option under the File menu to index the program back to an earlier quarter. So, for example, after your administrator processes your decisions for Quarter 1, when you load the *Threshold* program, it will automatically set up for your company's Quarter 2 decisions. To see how your company performed in Quarter 1 and to see the market research information you purchased, you will choose the Select Quarter option and enter a 1 as the desired quarter number. You will then be able to view or print the actual results of your decisions and market research information for Quarter 1. When you are ready to begin entering your Quarter 2 decisions, choose the Select Quarter option again and enter a 2 as the quarter number.

USING A HARD DISK

If you have a hard disk, you can choose to copy the files from your company disk to a directory on your hard drive and work from that directory to make your decisions. However, we believe it is best to work with the company disk. You need to turn in your company's decisions for each quarter to your administrator using your company disk. It is simpler to do this if you are working directly with your company disk. Otherwise, you will need to copy the *Threshold* THR.DAT file from the hard disk back onto your company disk before you hand it in. Once the *Threshold* program has been loaded, the program will quickly accept the decisions you enter and display reports (either forecasts or actuals) on your computer's screen. What time you save by operating the *Threshold* program on your hard disk is most likely lost when transferring files between your company disk and your hard disk.

Certainly, you can choose to work off of your hard disk, but **make sure you do not accidentally forget to transfer your decisions from your hard disk to your company disk**. *You* are responsible for the accuracy of the decisions you turn in to your administrator, *not* the administrator! If you forget to transfer your decisions to your company disk, you will have to live with the consequences of this mistake, which could be severe. Just as in business, you have to be responsible for the mistakes you make, not someone else.

If you do choose to work off of your hard disk, use one of the following sets of directions to copy the proper files to and from the hard disk and your company disk.

<u>If you are using the DOS Version of *Threshold*</u>.
1. Make a directory in which to store your *Threshold* files. To do this, at the C> type in **MD\THRW** and press [ENTER]. Note, you will have to do this only for the first time you create the *Threshold* directory on a particular machine. Thereafter, you can skip this step and start with Step 2b.

2a. If this is the first time you are using *Threshold* on the hard disk on this machine, copy all the files on your company disk to your hard disk. To do this, put your company disk in Drive A and type in **XCOPY A:*.* C:\THRW** and press [ENTER].
2b. If you have earlier copied your *Threshold* files to your hard drive, update your hard drive files by copying the thr.dat file to the Thresh hard drive directory. To do this, at the C> type in **COPY A:THR.DAT C:\THRW** and press [ENTER].
3. Change to the your *Threshold* directory. To do this, at the C> type in **CD\THRW** and press [ENTER].
4. At the C:\THRW>, type in **THR** and press [ENTER]. This will load the *Threshold* program. Enter your decisions as described earlier in this chapter.
5. When you are finished entering decisions, exit the program using the Exit option under the File heading on the Menu Bar.
6. Copy your company's data file onto your company disk, which is in Drive A. To do this. type in **COPY C:\THRW\THR.DAT A:** and press [ENTER].

If you are using the Windows Version.
1. If you have not yet loaded the *Threshold* Windows files, follow the directions for doing so under the section on "Starting the *Threshold* Program" described earlier in this chapter.
2. Using either the File Manager (for Windows 3.1x) or Explorer (for Windows 95 or Windows NT), copy the THR.DAT file from your company disk in Drive A to the THRW directory created during your Windows setup. (If you do not know how to do this, click on the MS DOS icon. At the DOS prompt, type in **A:THR.DAT C:\THRW** and press [ENTER]. Then exit the DOS prompt and return to the Windows environment.)
3. Double-click on the *Threshold* Company icon to start the *Threshold* program. Enter your decisions as described earlier in this chapter.
4. When you are finished entering decisions, exit the program using the Exit option under the File heading on the Menu Bar.
5. Using either the File Manager (for Windows 3.1x) or Explorer (for Windows 95 or Windows NT), copy the THR.DAT file from your THRW directory to the company disk in Drive A. (If you do not know how to do this, click on the MS DOS icon. At the DOS prompt, type in **COPY C:\THRW\THR.DAT A:** and press [ENTER]. Then exit the DOS prompt and return to the Windows environment.)

Labeling the *Threshold* Icon. If you choose to work off of your hard disk and you are working in a Windows environment, you can use the *Threshold* icon that the program created when you used the Windows setup process described earlier. You can create your own label name for this icon using one of the two following options. But first, single-click on the icon that you want to label so that it is highlighted. It should look similar to Exhibit 4.19.

Exhibit 4.19

- If you are working in Windows 3.1x, select the Properties option under the File menu in the Program Manager. A dialogue box similar to Exhibit 4.20 will appear on your screen. Type in the new label name you desire in the "Description" box and click on OK

Exhibit 4.20

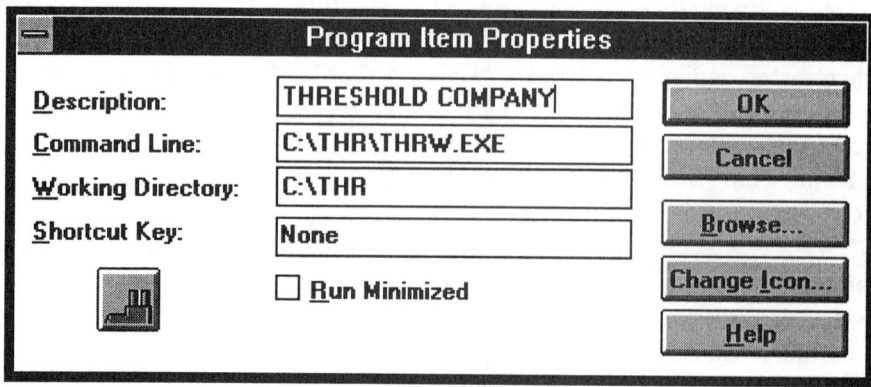

- If you are working in Windows 95 or Windows NT, make sure the icon you want to label is highlighted. Press the right-click button on your mouse and a dialogue box similar to Exhibit 4.21 will appear on your screen.

Exhibit 4.21

Select the Rename option and type in the new label you desire. Finally, left-click anywhere outside the icon.

MAKING A BACKUP DISK

You should always keep a backup of your company disk to protect against unexpected damage or loss of the disk. **It is your responsibility to protect your company's assets! This includes your company disk!** Just because you are careful does not mean nothing can, or will, go wrong. Bad luck does happen. It is up to you to protect against it.

Failure to properly maintain a backup of your disk can have severe consequences. It is extremely important to make backups regularly. This will protect you in case your main disk is damaged in any way. Remember Murphy's Law: "If anything can go wrong, it will, and at the worst possible time."

To make a backup copy of your company disk, you can use either the DOS diskcopy command or the similar command using the File Manager under your Program Manager options if you have Windows 3.1x on your computer. If you are using Windows 95 or Windows NT, use the Windows Explorer program and select the Send To option under the File Menu. Select one of these options after you have exited the *Threshold* program.

Making a Backup Disk Using DOS Commands

If you choose to use the DOS diskcopy option, at either the A> prompt or the C> prompt, type in **diskcopy a: a:**, press [ENTER] and follow the directions that appear on your screen.

The instructions will tell you to place your SOURCE disk in Drive A. The SOURCE disk is your company disk. Press [ENTER] when it is in the drive. You will have to wait while the computer reads the information on your disk. Once it has finished reading your disk, the instructions will next tell you to place your TARGET disk in the drive. The TARGET disk is a blank disk that you will use for a backup. Press [ENTER] when it is in the drive. Depending on the configuration of your computer, you may be asked to put the Source disk back in the drive for a second time so that the computer can complete reading all of the information on your company disk. It will then ask you to put the Target disk in the drive for a second time as well. You will know the computer has completed the copy process when you are asked if you want to copy another disk. If you do, press **Y** and follow the directions on the screen to repeat the process described above. Otherwise press **N** to return to the DOS prompt, either A> or C>.

Making a Backup Disk Using Windows

If you are working in Windows, you can make a backup copy of your company disk by using File Manager programs for Windows 3.1x or the Explorer programs for Windows 95 or Windows NT. If you are using Windows 3.1x, click on the File Manager icon which can usually be found under the "Main" program group. Select the Copy Disk option from under the Disk heading on the Menu Bar and follow the instructions shown on the screen. If you are using Windows 95 or Windows NT, click on My Computer and highlight the icon labeled "3½ floppy [A:]". Then select the Copy Disk option from under the File heading and follow the directions.

Once you have completed making a backup copy of your team's disk, place a label on it entitled *Threshold* Backup. The next time you use *Threshold*, use this disk again as your backup. You may want to store your working company disk and any backup disks in two separate locations. If anything happens to your company disk so that it is not usable, use the backup disk instead. If you have to use your backup disk, be sure to create another backup disk immediately, just to be safe. Remember, bad luck can strike twice in the same place.

TROUBLE SHOOTING

The *Threshold* program has undergone literally hundreds of hours of testing, both inside and outside the classroom. However, it is always wise for you to be prepared for "What do I do if ....?" or "What do I do now?" situations.

Complete System Failure

The first thing to remember is that even if the computer system suddenly fails to operate (frequently referred to as a "crash"), the data on your company disk will not be destroyed. In this worst-case scenario, restart the *Threshold* program. Any entries you had already saved will still be on your company disk. If you have not yet saved your decisions, you will have to re-enter them.

***Threshold* Program Failure**

Periodically, a sector of a disk becomes worn from high use or damaged by a disk drive as it reads from and writes to the disk. If the *Threshold* program file fails to load because of disk damage, your administrator can restore your company files by re-creating your company disk. See your administrator to do this or use your backup disk, if you have been keeping it up to date.

Viruses

The danger of a virus contaminating your company disk and disabling the files stored on it is ever-present. If your *Threshold* program will not operate, it may be the result of a virus infection. Run a virus check of your company disk to see if this has occurred. **If your disk has a virus on it, do NOT try to use it in another machine without first removing the virus.** If you do not know how to do this, get help! Any continued use of the disk will only spread the virus to more computers.

It is your responsibility to keep your company disk free of viruses. You would be wise to scan your disk for viruses *every* time you use it and before you turn it in to your administrator. Not doing this leaves you exposed to virus infections. Assume the worst whenever you use a computer that others have used. Your administrator may choose to impose a large fine on your company if you turn in a disk that is infected with a virus.

Data Entry Errors

If you attempt to make data entries that are outside acceptable limits, you will receive an error message from the *Threshold* program. Press the ESC Key to cancel the illegal entry and try again. Remember, you can change your entries as often as you like *before* your administrator has processed your decisions. This is discussed in detail in Chapter 5 under the Sales Forecast heading.

RE-PROCESS A PREVIOUS QUARTER

This option is only used in very rare instances where it is necessary to make changes in decisions that have already been processed. Your administrator will decide when it must be used. If your administrator instructs you to repeat a previous quarter, use the Select Quarter option under the File menu heading. Enter the quarter number told to you by your administrator that is going to be re-processed. Next, select the Decision menu heading. Notice that there is now a third option under that heading: "Change Decisions." Exhibit 4.22 shows an example of what this screen will look like.

Chapter 4, Using the Company Disk 41

Exhibit 4.22

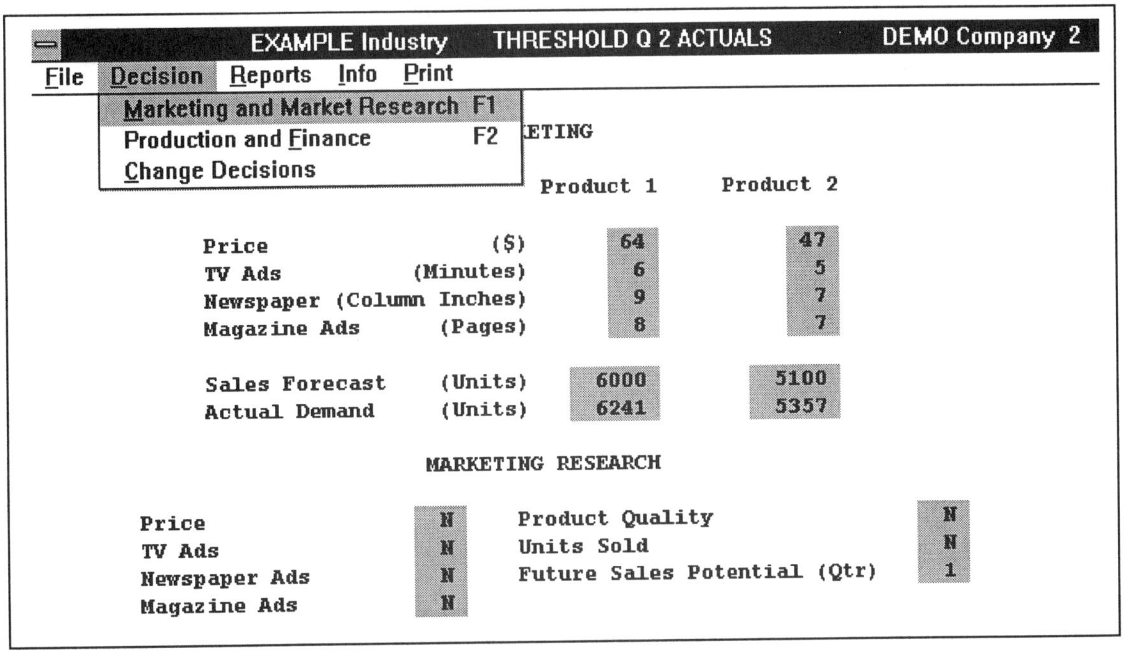

```
         EXAMPLE Industry    THRESHOLD Q 2 ACTUALS         DEMO Company 2
File  Decision  Reports  Info  Print
      Marketing and Market Research  F1
      Production and Finance          F2    ETING
      Change Decisions
                                             Product 1      Product 2

              Price            ($)              64             47
              TV Ads           (Minutes)         6              5
              Newspaper (Column Inches)          9              7
              Magazine Ads     (Pages)           8              7

              Sales Forecast   (Units)        6000           5100
              Actual Demand    (Units)        6241           5357

                              MARKETING RESEARCH

         Price             N        Product Quality                  N
         TV Ads            N        Units Sold                       N
         Newspaper Ads     N        Future Sales Potential (Qtr)     1
         Magazine Ads      N
```

When you select that option, *Threshold* will ask for a password (See Exhibit 4.23). Enter the password your administrator has given you. You will then be able to enter new decisions for that quarter.

Exhibit 4.23

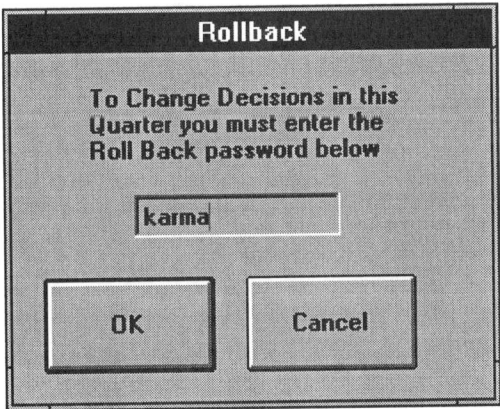

If you enter the wrong password, a dialogue box will appear on your monitor telling you that you entered the wrong password. (See Exhibit 4.24). If you do not enter the correct password, you will not be allowed to enter decisions for that quarter.

Exhibit 4.24

Do not attempt to make changes on your own without the administrator's approval. Even if you succeed in doing so, the records your administrator keeps in the administrator's files will override your changes, put your company records in turmoil, and make successful completion of the simulation extremely difficult.

You should now be familiar with the mechanics of working with *Threshold*. Go on to Chapter 5. We will discuss the decisions you have available to you to manage your *Threshold* company.

CHAPTER 5

MAKING DECISIONS

OVERVIEW OF DECISIONS

Your team needs to make and enter decisions in five main areas:
- marketing
- production
- finance
- sales forecasting
- management dilemmas

These five areas of decisions appear on the two decisions screens that you previewed in Chapter 4. In this chapter we will describe each decision for each of those five areas. Refer back to Chapter 4 if you are uncertain how to enter the decisions on the screens. This chapter will discuss the content of the decision, not the process for entering it.

THE BUSINESS PLAN

Before making any decisions, your management team should develop a business plan for your company. This is an important first step to help you cohesively tie together all your decisions. Without this plan, various parts of your business could be working against each other. For example, your marketing manager might have developed a marketing plan designed to sell a high volume of both products. At the same time, your operations manager may have developed a production plan with a goal of constraining production to avoid overtime and minimize costs. This could result in stimulating more demand for your products than you had available to sell. This would result in lost sales, which would mean lost income and unhappy customers. Developing a business plan can help you avoid parts of your company working toward conflicting goals. You will use your business plan to guide you in the marketing, operations, and financial decisions you have to make.

Chapter 2 discusses the steps of the planning process: creating a mission statement, statement of goals, strategies, and policies. Reread that chapter to guide your team in the development of your company's business plan. Once you have made this plan, your team is ready to begin to make the specific decisions described in this chapter.

Developing a Business Plan

As discussed in Chapter 2, the first step of the planning process is to develop a mission statement for your company. Let us consider two very different company missions. One would be to meet the customer need for a premier quality product that is relatively price inelastic. For customers buying this product, quality, not price, drives their decision-making process. The opposite focus would be to meet the customer need for a low-priced product where quality is less important. This does not mean that quality is unimportant, but is a secondary issue after price.

These two different company missions would result in two very different strategies. The high-quality focus would lead to a differentiation strategy, while the low price focus would lead to a low-cost strategy. Regardless of which strategy you choose to pursue, you will face the same sets of decisions in marketing, operations, and finance. However, the nature of the decisions you make will be very different. For example, you will need to make marketing decisions about price, quality, and promotional support for the sale of your product. A differentiation strategy will naturally lead to high investments in the quality of the product to support the marketing efforts. A cost strategy will of necessity result in efforts to lower the company's cost of operations so that the company can maintain profits even though its product's price is much lower than that of companies with a differentiation strategy. This will make the cost of production a critical concern for companies pursuing the cost strategy. Efficient operations (e.g., plant utilization, worker utilization and productivity, and inventory control), while important to every company, will be a key to achieving success for those companies taking the low-price/low-cost route to the marketplace. Managing your financial requirements to minimize unnecessary financial charges will also be important to pursuers of a cost strategy.

Keep these issues in mind as you read about the different decisions you will have to make to manage your *Threshold* company. We will now discuss in detail the decisions you will make each quarter.

MARKETING DECISIONS

For each quarter, you will have a variety of marketing decisions to make. These decisions will include:
- pricing
- advertising (i.e., TV, newspaper, and magazine)
- market research information (i.e., demand forecasts and competitor activities)

In addition to those marketing decisions, you will make sales forecasts of the number of units of Products 1 and 2 that you expect to sell that quarter. You will make this forecast based on your company's marketing effort, your expectations of your competitors' marketing efforts, and your knowledge of the overall market demand for each of the products.

You should also include in your sales forecast your expectation of the impact of your product's quality on sales. The combination of a product's price and quality creates a value to the customer. This value, combined with your promotional efforts (e.g., advertising), will influence sales of your product. How much you choose to spend on building quality into your products is one of your production decisions. We will discuss the production decisions later in this chapter.

You will enter each of your marketing decisions on the Marketing and Market Research decisions screen (Exhibit 4.2, Chapter 4). We will now discuss each of these decisions in detail below.

Price

In *Threshold*, companies operate in an oligopoly. This means relatively few companies manufacture a major portion of the total number of products produced and sold in their industry. In this industry, price is of major importance to the customer. The small number of companies offering products for sale makes it easy for potential customers to be aware of price differences in the marketplace. If a company prices its product higher than its competitors', customers will buy the lower-priced product unless they are enticed by stronger marketing efforts, a better quality product, or both.

The price of your product affects sales in two ways. The position of your price compared to that of your competitors has the biggest effect on your level of sales. Considering price alone, a product priced at $70 will sell more than one priced at $71. In addition, a change in price from last quarter also has an effect on how much you will sell. All other things being equal, if you just raised your price, you will sell less than if you had kept price constant from one quarter to the next. If you just lowered your price, you will sell more. The bigger the change in price, the bigger the effect of the price change on demand for your product.

Television Advertisements

A second factor that affects demand for your products is television ads. Each company has the option of purchasing up to 99 minutes of advertising for its products on the local television station. You can also choose to place no TV ads for your products. Enter a number from 0 to 99 for each product. The more minutes of advertising time your team purchases *relative to other companies in the industry*, the higher the demand will be for your company's product. However, there is a point of diminishing returns and also a point of saturation. You should not assume that very large amounts of television advertising are necessarily more effective than lesser amounts.

Newspaper Advertisements

Your company can also advertise in a local newspaper. For each quarter of operation, you must decide how many column inches (from 0 to 99) of advertising space you wish to purchase. Each newspaper ad that you purchase will run once a week for the 13 weeks of the quarter. So if you enter a 12 for this decision, it means you have purchased an ad that is 12 column inches in length that will run once each week for the next 13 weeks. Like television advertising, newspaper advertising will tend to increase demand for your product, *to a point*. Determining where these diminishing returns begin to take effect is a puzzle for your team to solve. This is a problem that all companies in the simulation exercise face, just as real companies in the real world do. Regardless of whether you are managing General Motors, Kelly's Auto Repairs, or a *Threshold* company, all companies face the question of "How much advertising is enough, and how much is too much?".

Magazine Advertisements

Another factor affecting demand is magazine advertisements. You have the option of purchasing from 0 to 99 full-page ads in popular, general-audience magazines selling in your market area. A point of diminishing returns also exists for this promotional media. A proper advertising campaign used with a market research program should try to identify this point.

Unlike television or newspaper ads, magazine advertisements also have an impact on sales that carries over to the next quarter. This is because people often save magazines and read them later and because they pass magazines on to others to read. This delayed reading causes a secondary effect on product sales. Thus, demand is affected by the number of magazine ads you purchased this quarter, plus the number of magazine ads placed last quarter.

SALES FORECAST ESTIMATE

The *Threshold* simulation allows companies to make a forecast of how much of each product participants think they will sell in that quarter of operation. Enter a number between 0 and 99,999 for both Product 1 and Product 2 that is your best estimate of the sales volume you will achieve for each product. Base your estimate on your marketing mix of pricing, advertising, and the investment in product quality (discussed below) you have chosen to make this quarter. You need to adjust this estimate for what you expect your competitors to do, the *Threshold* economic climate, and general demand for the product.

Once you enter the forecasts, the *Threshold* program uses those numbers to generate forecast reports that show what would happen if you actually sold the amount you forecasted. These forecast reports allow you to see what your operating costs and net income would be, whether you need to request a short-term loan, and what your overall financial picture would be for the quarter. You can also see what your material inventories would be and what the cost of producing your products would be that quarter.

Take note. These reports are *forecast* reports, and are labeled accordingly on the report screens and any printouts you generate. They are only as good as your estimate of the demand for your products. No guarantee exists that you will actually sell what you forecast. Actual sales are determined after your instructor has processed your decisions along with the decisions of the other companies in your industry. At that time the reports are labeled as "actual" reports to distinguish them from the forecasted reports. If you have misjudged your competitors' actions or the general market demand for the two products, your forecasted sales can be considerably different from your actual sales. If this is the case, your forecasted results will not resemble your actual results. This means your ability to plan your actions and predict your results will be highly dependent upon your ability to forecast accurately.

Remember two things about your sales forecasts. First, the sales forecasts you enter have no effect on your actual sales in a quarter. The *Threshold* program does not consider sales forecasts when determining actual sales of a product. It only considers the pricing, promotion, quality, and total market demand for a product when allocating sales. Second, *Threshold* will not warn you that your sales forecasts are unrealistic. It is your responsibility to understand your marketplace, using both quantitative and intuitive skills, and make a reasoned determination of what will be your products' sales volumes.

As was discussed in Chapter 4, you can see these forecast reports by pressing [PgDn] or using one of the "hot" keys after entering all your decisions. After looking at the forecasted reports, you can modify your decision inputs to maximize your company's efficiency and performance. You can make as many modifications to your decision inputs as you wish. The decisions you have entered do not become "permanent" until your instructor has processed them. You can test any number of possible decision sets to determine which will yield the best results for your company.

Five factors – price, TV ads, newspaper ads, magazine ads, and investment in product quality – combine to determine what portion of the market each company will capture (i.e., its market share). The investment in product quality decision will be described later in this chapter under Production Decisions.

You should keep in mind three issues as you develop your marketing program. First, as with almost any product, the advertising of your *Threshold* products can reach a point of diminishing return. As you raise your levels of advertising, more potential customers become aware of your products. Unfortunately, awareness does not guarantee a purchase. At some point, additional expenditures on advertising will result in smaller increases in the number of sales of that product. Determining when you have reached this point is a problem all companies face and will be a continual challenge for your company. Second, if you spend too little on advertising, your efforts may result in few sales because your promotional efforts are overshadowed by your competitors' promotional efforts. Finally, if the whole industry spends little on promotion of the *Threshold* products, your potential customers will purchase substitute products sold by companies outside your *Threshold* industry. This would mean neither you nor your *Threshold* competitors would sell the sales potential forecasted for the industry. This can also occur if the whole industry invests too little in product quality. Your task then is to design a marketing program that is both effective and efficient. For a marketing program to be successful, it must generate the demand you desire at the lowest possible cost.

Exhibit 5.1 summarizes the information on marketing decisions and the range of numbers your team can enter for each decision. This information is repeated in Appendix E along with other important information. You can also access this information through the Info option on the Menu Bar or by using "hot" keys (Shift + F1).

EXHIBIT 5.1

THRESHOLD **LIMITS AND TIME LAGS**

MARKETING

Decision Variable	Range/ Limits	Lag Before Impact
Price ($)	0 - 99	Immediate
TV Ads (Minutes)	0 - 99	Immediate
Newspaper Ads (Column Inches)	0 - 99	Immediate
Magazine Ads (Pages)	0 - 99	Immediate
Sales Forecasts (Units)	0 - 99,999	No Impact

MARKET RESEARCH DECISIONS

Another set of marketing decisions deals with market research. You will enter these decisions on the Marketing and Marketing Research screen. You tell the computer whether you want to buy a market research report by entering **Y** for Yes or **N** for No.

Your company may choose to purchase up to seven different market research reports. These allow you to obtain information on your competitors as well as information on demand for the products in your industry. Your company can buy any or all of these reports each *Threshold* quarter and receive them *after* your instructor processes that quarter. Costs for these reports in Quarter 0 are shown in Exhibit 5.2 and in Appendix D. Costs for market information are subject to change during the simulation. The *Threshold* program stores current cost information on your company disk. You can access this information through the Info option on the Menu Bar or by pressing the F3 "hot" key. Your instructor has the option of changing these initial costs for Quarter 1. So you would be wise to check the costs on your company disk for any changes from those listed here. Appendix C is an example of what the market research reports you can purchase look like. We will discuss each of the market research reports that you can purchase next.

Price by Company

The first research report lists the selling price for both products for all companies operating in the industry. Since *Threshold* is an oligopoly, the demand for the products is heavily dependent on price. Therefore, this report can prove to be valuable as you assess the results of one quarter and make plans for the next quarter.

Television, Newspaper, Magazine, and Product Quality Reports

These four reports are quite similar. Each report lists the effort expended by each company in your industry for that particular issue. For example, if you purchase the market research on television advertising, you will receive a report showing the number of minutes of TV advertising purchased that quarter by each company for both of the products. If you purchase the product quality report, you will receive a report showing how much each company invested that quarter on product quality for each product.

Units Sold by Company

You will receive an Industry Performance Report without cost each quarter. We will discuss this report in Chapter 6. It tells the sales revenues for each competitor. However, you can also purchase a report showing the number of units sold of both products by each company.

Future Sales Potential

Future demand for a product is of major importance to an individual company. You can purchase a research report that shows future sales potential for the products up to four quarters in advance of the quarter in which you are operating. You can choose which of the next four quarters you want to buy, but you can buy information for only *one* quarter at a time. Enter the number of the quarter for which you want information on the Marketing and Marketing Research screen. If you enter the number of a quarter that is further out than four quarters, an error message will appear on your screen.

The former managers of your company purchased potential market demand for Quarter 1 in Quarter 0. You can see this report when you view the Market Research Report for Quarter 0 on the screen. The report shows that Quarter 1 demand will be 6,000 units for Product 1 and 5,100 units for Product 2. **These numbers do not represent the guaranteed sales volume for your company in Quarter 1**. They represent the average demand per company for the industry. Depending on your marketing effort relative to that of your competitors, you will sell above or below these levels. The numbers indicate how much each team would sell if the total market potential were divided equally among all teams in your industry. You can determine the total sales potential for a product by multiplying the number given in the research report by the number of teams in your industry. For example, if there are five teams in your industry, the total demand for Product 1 in Quarter 1 would be 30,000 units (i.e., 6,000 units x 5 teams). If one of your goals is to achieve a 25% share of the market for Product 1, your sales goal for Product 1 in Quarter 1 would be 7,500 units (30,000 x .25 = 7,500). This goal is greater than the average demand of 6,000 shown in the report, so to sell this amount requires a marketing effort greater than that of at least some of your competitors. Put simply, the more you want to sell above the average demand for a product, the greater effort you will have to put in to marketing your product relative to your competition. Remember, at some point the cost of this marketing effort will outweigh the benefits that come from the increased sales volume.

EXHIBIT 5.2
THRESHOLD MARKET RESEARCH COSTS

Market Research Information	Range/ Limits	Cost
Price ($)	By Company & Product	5,000
TV Ads (Minutes)	By Company & Product	5,000
Newspaper Ads (Column Inches)	By Company & Product	3,000
Magazine Ads (Pages)	By Company & Product	4,000
Product Quality ($)	By Company & Product	2,000
Sales (Units)	By Company & Product	5,000
Sales Potential	By Quarter & Product	10,000

You will have to decide what market research information is and is not valuable for managing your company. Careful use of this information can provide you with clues to the relative efficiency of your marketing efforts. You may also glean information on your competitors' strategies from these reports and use them to update your current strategies or to make decisions that preempt their competitive actions.

PRODUCTION DECISIONS

Production decisions you will make include:
- ordering raw material for each product.
- how much to invest in maintaining or enhancing the quality of your products.
- how many units of each product to make.
- the number of production workers to hire, fire, or lay off.
- whether to purchase or sell units of production capacity (i.e., plant capacity).
- how many dollars to invest in human resource development.

The production decisions you must make each quarter are entered on the Production and Finance screen. We will describe these decisions in more detail below.

Buy Raw Materials

Your company's products require one unit of the correct raw material for each unit of finished good produced and available for sale. Product 1 requires one kind of raw material, and Product 2 another. Companies must purchase the necessary raw materials for their production department. Enter the number of raw material units you wish to purchase for each product. Your purchasing department and your supplier require one full quarter to order and receive the material. This means you must purchase raw materials the quarter *before* you need them. There is no guarantee you will receive all the raw materials you order. There is a small chance that only 75% of an order for each raw material will actually arrive at your company's plant. Further, material costs may remain stable, decrease, or increase, reflecting a changing economy. This degree of risk forces advance planning. Check the Cost screen to determine the current price. If you order 15,000 units of a particular raw material, you will receive a quantity discount of 15% on the total cost of the materials purchased. The discount is not granted when the combined orders for both products total 15,000.

You cannot warehouse materials (either raw or finished goods) without cost. You incur a carrying charge for every unit of raw material remaining in inventory after the quarter's operations are completed. You will pay these carrying costs the next quarter. This means in Quarter 1 you will pay carrying charges for raw materials based on the inventory you had remaining at the end of Quarter 0. One problem you will face is the need to balance the cost of raw material delivery uncertainties against the cost of carrying an inventory of raw material as a safety stock. Your raw material policy should deal with these issues. The total cost of materials used in the production process will be the cost of the materials plus the cost of carrying any raw materials in inventory.

Investment in Product Quality

Each quarter you must choose how much money to spend to produce a quality product. Money spent on product quality will build into your product elements of quality important to the customer such as durability and appearance. These features will serve to differentiate your product from your competitors' and make them more attractive to potential customers. So, depending on how your pricing and advertising efforts compare with your competitors', improving the quality of your products will help increase the demand for them.

Money spent on product quality will also increase the cost of producing your products. This means you must increase the price of your product to recover the money spent on producing a quality product. Otherwise, you must increase your sales volume sufficiently to make your investment in product quality worthwhile. Determining the proper mix of price, quality, and sales volume will be a continuing conundrum for your company to resolve.

Diminishing returns can occur with product quality. At some point, the customer is satisfied with the quality of your product compared to your competitors' products and more dollars spent in this area may not be cost-effective. Remember, your customers will always be comparing the quality and the price of your product to that of your competition to see where they can get the "best buy". This means that even if you have spent money on product quality, your competition may sell more.

The money spent on producing a quality product only affects the products available for sale in the quarter in which the money is spent. This means money spent on producing a quality product in Quarter 1 will not affect the quality of the product produced in Quarter 2. Each quarter is independent of other quarters on this issue. If you want to maintain a level of product quality from one quarter to the next, you will have to spend a comparable amount of money in successive quarters. Enter a dollar figure from 0 to 99,999 for each of the two products for the amount you choose to spend on producing a quality product.

Number of Units to Produce

Three factors limit how much your plant can produce. You must have:
- the necessary raw materials available to produce a particular product,
- the plant capacity necessary to handle the combined production level of products P1 and P2 that you desire, and
- enough workers available to run the production equipment to produce the number of products you desire.

Raw Materials. You must decide how many units of each product you want to produce and enter the number (0 to 99,999) on the Production and Finance Screen. Since one unit of raw material makes one finished product, this is one factor controlling the volume that you can produce. Companies cannot produce more units of a product than they have of that product's type of raw material. If a company requests production in excess of raw material available, *Threshold* will set production at the total of available raw materials. For example, if you enter a production level of 1,000 units for Product 1 with only a 500-unit inventory of raw material for Product 1 available, then you can produce only 500 units of Product 1. You cannot substitute the raw materials for one of the two products for the other product. So, while you may have a large raw material inventory of Product 2, if you only have 500 units of raw material of Product 1 on hand, you can not produce more than 500 units of finished goods of Product 1.

Plant Capacity. Assuming you have the necessary number of raw materials available, you can produce more than plant capacity by working at overtime. The simulation limits overtime production to 150% of plant capacity. For example, with 11,100 units of plant capacity, maximum production allowed using maximum overtime is 16,650 units (11,100 * 150%). You pay an overtime charge for any units you produce at overtime. You will need to balance the cost of producing at overtime against the costs of lost sales because you did not produce enough to meet demand. This will help you to determine whether to purchase additional plant capacity (discussed below). Determining the cost of overtime is discussed later in a separate section.

Workers Available. How many units of each product you can produce is also limited by the number of workers you have available, *and* the current productivity levels of those workers. Your Labor Report (discussed in Chapter 6) will show how many workers you have available in the current quarter to manufacture Products 1 and 2. The current productivity levels of your workers are shown on the Cost Parameters Report. Determining whether you have too many or too few workers for the volume you want to produce is discussed in the "Workers to Hire, Fire, or Lay Off" section, below.

Overtime. *Threshold* automatically decides when overtime is needed to produce the volume you chose. You will be assessed overtime charges whenever you either (a) exceed 120% of your plant's capacity or (b) exceed the output your workers can produce *at their current productivity levels*. This means that even if you have enough capacity to produce 12,000 units, if your workers are only capable of producing 10,000 units at their current productivity rates, you will receive an overtime charge for all production above 10,000 units. The reverse of this also holds true. Your workers may be capable of producing 10,000 units, but if your current plant capacity is only 8,000 units, you will be assessed an overtime charge for all units produced above 9,600 units (8,000 * 120%). Notice that if you have enough workers, you can produce 20% above your plant's capacity without incurring overtime charges.

Threshold pays the workers the equivalent of *double time* for every unit they produce at overtime. To calculate your overtime rate, you must first calculate the average labor cost per unit *for each product*. Then determine the average of those two averages.

The following is an example of how to calculate the cost of producing at overtime in Quarter 1.
Given:
- Initial salary per worker per quarter is $4,000
- Initial worker productivity is 250 units for Product #1
- Initial worker productivity is 300 units for Product #2

Then:
- Average labor cost of Product 1 = $4000/250 = $16.00/unit
- Average labor cost of Product 2 = $4000/300 = $13.33/unit
- Average labor cost of Products 1 and 2 = ($16.00 + 13.33)/2 = $14.66/unit

Since overtime is charged at double normal rates, the cost per unit of overtime production is (14.66 * 2) or $29.32 per unit. Therefore, if you chose to produce 1,000 units at overtime, you would be assessed an overtime charge of $29,320 for those units.

You are not required to produce at plant capacity every quarter. Nor are you required to continue to produce both products. However, you will still incur the costs associated with the plant that you own even if it is not in use. These costs are the depreciation charges that reflect the aging of your plant and equipment. These costs are assigned to your cost of producing the two products in the same proportion that the two products are utilizing the plant. For example, if you produced 4,000 units of Product 1 and 6,000 units of Product 2, then 40% (4,000/[4,000 + 6,000]) of the plant's depreciation costs would be assigned to Product 1. You can see your quarterly depreciation charges on your company's Cost of Production report. We will discuss this report in some detail in Chapter 6. You will have to decide what production volume is best for your company.

Workers to Hire, Fire, or Lay Off

To manufacture a product, you must have the proper number of workers available to operate the equipment. Each quarter you will have to decide how many production workers to hire, fire, or lay off in order to maintain the number of workers you desire. Enter the number of each on the Production and Finance Screen. Each *Threshold* company will begin operation with 41 workers. Each worker can initially produce 250 units of Product 1 or 300 units of Product 2. *Threshold* will assign these workers to try to produce the number of each product that you request. For example, the current work force could produce 6,000 units of Product 1 (24 workers x 250 units/worker) and 5,100 units of Product 2 (17 workers x 300 units/worker) per quarter. These production levels would make 100% use of existing capacity (11,100 units) and utilize all the available workers, without incurring any overtime charges.

However, if you asked these same workers to produce 8,000 units of Product 1 and 3,100 units of Product 2 you would be charged overtime for the production of 400 units. This is because you need 32 of your 41 workers to produce the 8,000 units of Product 1 (8,000/250 = 32), leaving 9 workers to produce Product 2. Unfortunately, these 9 workers can only produce 2,700 units of Product 2 (9 workers x 300/worker). This means you need to produce the last 400 units (3,100 - 2,700) at overtime rates. As you can see from this example, workers are first assigned to produce Product 1 and then Product 2, to determine if overtime is needed to meet the desired production level.

You must hire production workers one quarter before you need them. Your human resources department requires one quarter to hire and train a worker at a cost of $2,000. Production workers can quit without notice. Historically you have lost 10% of your work force to turnover each quarter. Beyond this, there is a small random probability of losing an additional worker. Therefore, your company must develop a staffing strategy. The unplanned loss of workers can create a series of problems for your company. You should develop contingency plans to cope with this uncertainty.

You may choose to fire or lay off production workers. When you fire production workers, they are not available the quarter you discharge them. For example, a worker that you fire in Quarter 4 is discharged at the very beginning of the quarter and is not available to produce any product in Quarter 4. There is no charge for terminating production workers.

You may also decide to lay off workers for one quarter. A laid-off worker leaves at the beginning of the quarter and will return automatically at the beginning of the next quarter. The current cost attached to this method of work-force management is $500 for each worker laid off that quarter. A company must balance the cost of keeping a worker on layoff status against the cost of firing a worker and re-hiring a new person.

Buy or Sell Plant Capacity

Buy Plant Capacity. You have the option of purchasing additional plant capacity. This allows you to change the productive capacity of your physical plant. Additions to capacity are currently available for $45 per unit of production capacity. Enter the number of units of production capacity you want to buy on the Production and Finance screen. For example, for $45,000, management could increase capacity 1,000 units to 12,100 units per quarter. Planning the expansion is important because it will be one quarter before you can manufacture any additional products. If you order a plant in Quarter 1, you will bring it on-line and use it in Quarter 2. Remember that you may also need to hire production workers and order raw materials to use the added plant capacity.

Sell Plant Capacity. You can choose to sell capacity you no longer need. You sell plant capacity at book value (original cost minus accumulated depreciation). You can use the plant capacity the quarter you make the decision to sell it. The units are removed from the production process at the beginning of the next quarter. Collection of the money from the sale of the plant capacity also occurs at the beginning of the next quarter. For example, a request to sell 1,000 units of capacity in Quarter 2 will result in a 1,000 unit reduction in capacity at the beginning of Quarter 3. You can still use those 1,000 units for production in Quarter 2. You will receive the cash from this sale of plant in Quarter 3.

All capacity depreciates on a straight-line basis over 25 quarters. Therefore, depreciation expenses for any given quarter are 4% of the original cost of the capacity you own. This means the book value (i.e., sale price) of any plant you sell will be its purchase price minus 4% times the number of quarters it has been in operation. For example, if you sell plant that originally cost $100,000 and which has been used for five quarters, you would receive $80,000 (100,000 - [5 x .04 x 100,000] = 80,000).

You will always sell off your oldest plant first. This means if you added 1,000 units of plant capacity in Quarter 2 and then decided to sell 1,000 units in Quarter 5, you would be selling a plant that had been in use since Quarter 0, not the 1,000 units you just purchased in Quarter 2. Enter the number of units of production capacity you want to sell on the Production and Finance screen.

Human Resource Development

Investment in Human Resource Development is money spent in an effort to improve the productivity of your production workers. It includes training programs designed to improve employee skills and morale and increase the amount of finished goods product each worker can produce in a quarter. If this occurs, it can effectively lower the company's worker payroll costs. But, there is no guarantee that money spent in this area will translate into productivity increases. Nor is there a guarantee of how much the workers' productivity will increase, if an increase does occur. All that can be said for certain is that this investment may improve worker productivity. However, it is expected that the larger your company's investment in Human Resource Development, the greater the likelihood that the productivity of your workers will increase.

Similarly, little or no investment in Human Resource Development will most likely lead to lower worker productivity. This is because workers can become less efficient if there are no training programs to improve, or at least maintain, their skills. Workers also can become less motivated to produce up to their ability if they think management is not concerned about productivity.

To the extent that investments in Human Resource Development (HRD) do influence worker productivity, the effect occurs in the quarter *following* the one in which you made the investments. In addition, any investment in productivity lasts for only *one* quarter. For example, an investment in Human Resource Development in Quarter 1 may improve worker productivity in Quarter 2. Assuming that productivity increased to a new level, it will stay at that level, increase, or decrease in Quarter 3 depending on the amount of money invested in HRD in Quarter 2. Remember, there is no guarantee that a similar investment will result in a similar increase in productivity in subsequent quarters. However, history is often a good predictor of the future. Your company's policies and philosophy will affect your decision about how much your company will choose to invest in Human Resource Development. Enter a dollar figure from 0 to 99,999 as your decision.

Exhibit 5.3 and Appendix E show the ranges within which your production decisions must occur and the time dimensions associated with each decision. Notice that for many of these decisions, there is a one quarter lag before the decisions take effect. For example, when you order raw materials for your products this quarter, you will not actually receive the materials until next quarter. This means you will need to plan ahead for items that have a time lag associated with them. Note that the Quarter 0 Reports in Appendix B show the results of a number of decisions made by your company's owners prior to Quarter 0 so that production could occur in Quarter 0. These included hiring production workers (45) and ordering raw materials (6,500 units for Product 1 and 5,500 units for Product 2).

EXHIBIT 5.3
THRESHOLD LIMITS AND TIME LAGS
PRODUCTION

Decision Variable	Range/ Limits	Lag Before Impact
Buy Raw Material (#) (Products 1 & 2)	0 - 99,999	1 Quarter
Invest in Product Quality ($)	0 - 99,999	Immediate
Units Produced (#) (Products 1 & 2)	0 - 99,999	Immediate
Workers Hired for Next Quarter (#)	0 - 99	1 Quarter
Workers Fired This Quarter (#)	0 - 99	Immediate
Workers Laid Off This Quarter (#)	0 - 99	Immediate
Purchase Plant Capacity (# of Units)	0 - 40,000	1 Quarter
Sell Plant Capacity (# of Units)	0 - 99,999	1 Quarter
Human Resource Development ($)	0 - 99,999	1 Quarter

FINANCE DECISIONS

You must make three types of financial decisions:
- short-term loan requests to finance your current operations,
- long-term mortgages to finance purchases of plant capacity,
- short-term investment deposits of cash from operations or withdrawals from prior short-term investments.

Enter these decisions on the Production and Finance screen. We will discuss each of these decisions in detail, below.

Short-Term Loans

Your company must perform some basic financial activities to conduct the operation of its business. Short-term financing is available to cover cash shortages you might encounter in your normal business operations. This is money you need to cover the costs of the marketing and production decisions you make. Enter the dollar figure of the short-term loan you want. You must forecast your need for money and plan for these shortages. No *Threshold* company is allowed to operate with a negative cash balance. If a company does not forecast cash accurately and ends the quarter with a negative cash balance, the *Threshold* bank will automatically provide that company with an emergency loan for the amount of money necessary to bring the company up to a zero balance. The penalty for this service is double the normal short-term interest rates on the total amount of loan needed for that quarter. This means if you needed $50,000 to finance operations in a quarter, but requested a short-term loan of only $40,000, the interest penalty would be charged on the $50,000 needed, **not** on the $10,000 you were short in your request. Companies who accurately forecast cash will not be subject to this interest penalty. This means you do not want to request a short-term loan that is likely to fall short of your actual cash needs after your decisions have been processed. At the same time, you do not want to request a short-term loan far in excess of your actual cash needs either. If you do, you will end up paying interest charges on money that is sitting idle in your cash account and not "working" to generate profits for your company. Your goal should always be to have the expenses associated with borrowing money (i.e., interest expenses) be less than the profits generated by the use of that money. Money sitting idle in your cash account neither earns any interest income nor generates any profits for your company.

Any short-term loan money you borrow at the end of a quarter must be completely repaid during the next quarter of operation. This means the $310,000 short-term loan borrowed in Quarter 0 will be repaid in Quarter 1. There is a limit on how much you can borrow short-term in any quarter. Initially the most your *Threshold* banker will lend you on a short-term basis is $800,000. This credit limit can change over time, depending on your company's performance. The administrator may also choose to set different limits. It is up to you to make certain the *Threshold* banker will accept your loan request. If your loan request is denied, you could end up receiving an expensive emergency loan.

Long-Term Mortgages

Request. To gain funds for capital investments, such as plant additions, companies typically use long-term mortgages. You must finance normal operating expenses (i.e., advertising costs or labor costs) through short-term loan requests. The *Threshold* bank requires you to repay all long-term mortgages in equal installments over 25 quarters. You may request new mortgage loans in addition to any you presently have outstanding. The total dollar amount of mortgages you can have outstanding will be limited by your *Threshold* banker. Interest rates on these mortgages will be the prevailing rate set by the bank. Any funds approved in response to a request for a new mortgage will be added to the outstanding balance of any existing mortgage.

Extra Payment. If you so choose, you can make extra payments to reduce the outstanding balance on your mortgage. Reducing the amount of your mortgage will reduce the interest charges associated with it. You will have to determine whether to use any of the extra cash your company has generated to pay down your mortgage balance or for some other purpose.

Short-Term Investments

Deposits. You may forecast that your company will end up with excess cash after paying this quarter's bills. If so, you may choose to invest that money in short-term marketable securities. The company's Board of Directors has dictated that you purchase only the most stable securities. Consequently, earnings are relatively low compared to interest rates for higher risk alternatives. Enter the amount of the short-term investment you wish to make on the Production and Finance screen. This amount can range from 0 to 999,999 as your decision.

The timing of this investment is immediate: Any money deposited into short-term investments is immediately deducted from your cash account. If you over-estimate the cash you will have at the end of the quarter and deposit so much into short-term investments that you end up needing cash, you will be forced to take an emergency loan at double the current short-term loan rates. This is because (as discussed earlier) *Threshold* does not allow you to have a negative cash balance at the end of a quarter's operations. Although you may have funds in your investment account, the marketable securities require that you formally request a withdrawal before any funds can be released and transferred to your cash account at your bank. Funds from your investment account will not be transferred automatically if your cash position is negative. So be careful! You need to forecast cash accurately even when you are cash rich. Investing more money than you have in your cash account can mean receiving a *Threshold* bank loan at rates much higher than your investment rates, which is not a prudent financial decision.

The bank pays you interest for any money you have invested the quarter after you make a short-term investment. Earnings from investments reduce the overall interest expenses of the company. This means interest income you earn from investments is credited against interest expense you owe for money you have borrowed. This will be reflected in the "Net Interest" line on your Income Statement and the "Net Short-Term Interest" line on your Cash Flow Statement.

If your interest income exceeds your interest expense, your net interest figure will show as a negative number. This will have the effect of adding to the company's operating profit rather than subtracting from it. It will also reduce the total cash payments figure on the company's Cash Flow Statement.

Withdrawals. You can withdraw money you have previously invested in short-term marketable securities. As noted above, you must formally request the withdrawal of funds from your investment account before the securities are deposited as cash in your bank account. While this precludes the use of short-term investments to prevent emergency loans, any funds withdrawn will arrive in your cash account in sufficient time to be used as part of the cash available to meet that quarter's expenses.

Exhibit 5.4 and Appendix E show the financial decisions you have to make and the fact that all of the financial decisions take effect immediately.

EXHIBIT 5.4
THRESHOLD LIMITS AND TIME LAGS
FINANCE

Decision Variable	Range/ Limits	Lag Before Impact
Short-Term Loan Requested ($)	0 - 9,999,999 *	Immediate
Mortgage Request ($)	0 - 9,999,999	Immediate
Extra Payment ($)	0 - 999,999	Immediate
Short-Term: Investment ($)	0 - 999,999	Immediate
Withdrawal ($)	0 - 999,999	Immediate

* initially $800,000

MANAGEMENT DILEMMAS

The *Threshold* simulation may force you to make some interesting and difficult decisions concerning your workers and your relationship with the local community. In Appendix G are a number of dilemmas that you may face. Issues include employee theft, incompetence, bribery, alcohol abuse, and union relations. Your instructor will notify you if and when you must address any of these dilemmas. If you need to make a dilemma decision, enter your decision on the bottom of the Production and Finance Screen. For each dilemma, there are several numbered options shown in Appendix G. Select from among these options, given your perception of the situation you are facing and the possible consequences for your company. There is not only one necessarily correct response, just different ones. In fact, your company could select the same option as another company, yet face different consequences from that decision. When dealing with human behavior, different people respond differently to the same actions. The ability to make good decisions where there are no clear answers is one of the critical skills needed by all managers. The consequences of your decisions can affect worker productivity, sales, cost of raw materials, or interest rates.

COST PARAMETERS REPORT

Exhibit 5.5 lists the costs and productivity figures for your Quarter 0 decisions. You can also find these costs on the Menu Bar under the Info heading or by pressing the F3 "hot" key. You will receive a printout of these costs whenever you request a printout of all pages of your company reports. You can do this by selecting the All Pages option under Print on the Menu Bar. You can also choose to print just the cost page using the Selected Screens option on the Print menu. You should check your company's cost parameters regularly for any unannounced changes. Any of the costs can change during the course of the *Threshold* exercise. It is possible that your costs for Quarter 1 may be different than those in effect for Quarter 0. Get in the habit of checking your current costs every quarter. It is up to you to be knowledgeable regarding your company's costs. Do not expect your instructor to always inform you of changes that have occurred to the cost of operating your company. Not recognizing which costs have changed will be detrimental to your ability to manage you company efficiently.

EXHIBIT 5.5

```
UNKNOWN Industry    THRESHOLD Q 0 ACTUALS         DEMO Company 0
File  Decision  Reports  Info  Print

                       COST PARAMETERS REPORT

                                      Product 1     Product 2

             Raw Material                 8.00         12.00
             Raw Material Warehouse       1.00          2.00
             Finished Goods Warehouse     2.50          1.50
             Worker Productivity           250           300

Television Ad Minutes         $    5000    Mkt Research-Product Price    $    5000
Newspaper Ad Column Inches    $    1000    Mkt Research-TV ADs Minutes   $    5000
Magazine Ad Pages             $    3000    Mkt Research-Newspaper Ads    $    3000
Workers' Quarterly Wages      $    4000    Mkt Research-Magazine Ads     $    4000
Hiring Costs per Worker       $    2000    Mkt Research-Product Quality  $    2000
Layoff Costs per Worker       $     500    Mkt Research-Unit Sales       $    5000
Administrative Expenses       $   12000    Mkt Research-Market Demand    $   10000
New Plant Cost per Unit       $      45    Manufacturing Overhead Rate   %    50.0
Short-Term Loan Rate          %    10.0    Mortgage Interest Rate        %     9.0
Short-Term Investment Rate    %     5.0
```

Appendix J provides a flow chart of the decisions you will make and how they lead to the forecast and actual reports you will use to manage your *Threshold* company. In the next chapter, we will discuss in some detail each of the reports available in *Threshold* that you will use to assess your company's performance and determine what future actions you wish to take in the managing of your *Threshold* company.

CHAPTER 6

THRESHOLD REPORTS

After your instructor processes each set of decisions, you will receive a number of reports that will show, in detail, the results of those decisions. You can view these reports and those of previous quarters using the Select Quarter option under File on the Main Menu. See Chapter 4 for a discussion of the process for viewing and printing reports. Remember, when you load up the *Threshold* program, it automatically loads up the *next* quarter's decision screens and associated reports. If you want to access the quarter that was just processed, you will have to use the Select Quarter option to move back to those reports.

In Chapter 6 we will provide a description of each *Threshold* report that you can access on your company disk. Appendix B contains the Quarter 0 reports for the start of the simulation. The reports include:
- operations reports
- selling and administrative expense reports
- income statement
- balance sheet
- cash flow statement

OPERATIONS REPORTS

Four of the *Threshold* reports show the current status of your manufacturing operations. These reports show the cost of manufacturing finished products that you made available for sale to your prospective customers.

Inventory Reports

The first two operations reports in Appendix B show the inventory levels for Products 1 and 2, respectively. The top of the Inventory Report shows the Raw Materials inventory levels for Products 1 and 2 (see Exhibit 6.1). The report for Quarter 0 shows a Beginning Balance of zero for both Products 1 and 2. At the start of Quarter 0, no units of raw material were available from last quarter's operations. The second line of the report shows how many units of raw materials were received in Quarter 0 and their total dollar value. The Units Received combined with the units in the Beginning Balance yield the Total Available raw materials. This is shown in both units and total dollar value. This shows the number of units that could be used to produce finished goods. A total of 6,500 units of raw materials were received in Quarter 0 for Product 1 and 5,500 for Product 2. Adding the beginning zero balance for both of the products results in total available raw material of 6,500 units worth $52,000 for Product 1 and 5,500 units worth $66,000 for Product 2.

Exhibit 6.1
Inventory Report

```
UNKNOWN Industry      THRESHOLD Q 0 ACTUALS          DEMO Company 0
File  Decision  Reports  Info  Print

RAW MATERIAL                       Product 1              Product 2
INVENTORY REPORT         Units           Value    Units           Value

Beginning Balance           0               0        0               0
Units Received           6500           52000     5500           66000
Total Available          6500           52000     5500           66000
Used in Production       6000           48000     5100           61200
Ending Balance            500            4000      400            4800
Raw Matl Warehouse Costs    0               0        0               0
Total Product Cost                      48000                    61200

FINISHED GOODS                     Product 1              Product 2
INVENTORY REPORT         Units  $/Unit  Value    Units  $/Unit  Value

Beginning Balance           0    .00        0        0    .00       0
Production               6000  37.42   224526     5100  40.23  205154
Units to Sell            6000  37.42   224526     5100  40.23  205154
Units Sold               6000  37.42   224526     5100  40.23  205154
End Balance                 0    .00        0        0    .00       0
FG Warehouse                0   2.50        0        0   1.50       0
Lost Sales                  0  64.00        0        0  47.00       0
```

The fourth line shows the number of units of raw material that were used in the production process that quarter and their dollar value. Reports for Quarter 0 show production of 6,000 of Product 1 units valued at $48,000. That leaves a raw material Ending Balance of 500 units valued at $4,000.

The Raw Material Warehouse Costs reflect the cost of carrying units of raw material in inventory from one quarter to the next. Since no inventory was carried over from the previous quarter, there are no warehouse costs associated with raw materials for either product this quarter.

The last line of the Raw Materials section of the Inventory Report shows the Total Cost of the raw materials for Product 1 that were put into the production process. This figure includes the cost of the material itself plus the cost of carrying raw materials in inventory. Since there were no carrying costs in Quarter 0, the total cost of raw materials charged to the production process for Product 1 equaled $48,000, or just the cost of the raw material for Product 1. If there are inventory costs in a quarter, they are added to the cost of raw material.

The bottom of the Inventory Report shows the Finished Goods warehouse operations for both products. The columns show the number of units, the per unit cost, and the total value of that item. The first line shows the Beginning Balance of finished goods remaining in inventory from last quarter. This line shows the number of units not sold last quarter that are available for sale this quarter. At the beginning of Quarter 0, no finished goods remained in inventory.

The next line, Production, indicates the production level for the quarter. This is the number of units of raw material that were converted into finished goods. The per unit cost reflects all the costs of manufacturing Products 1 and 2 (i.e., the cost of materials, labor, overhead, etc.) to make them ready for sale to prospective customers. In Quarter 0, 6,000 units of raw material for Product 1 produced finished products at a cost of $37.42 per unit. The cost elements that go into that $37.42 will be discussed in the Cost of Production report below.

The next line, Units to Sell, shows the number of finished units available for sale over the course of the quarter. This is the combination of the beginning balance and the units produced for the quarter. The line also shows the per unit cost and the total value of these finished units.

The number of units that were sold during the quarter are shown next. The Ending Balance line shows the number of units remaining in finished goods inventory after that quarter's sales have been made. All the units available for sale for both products were sold, so at the end of Quarter 0, no finished goods remained for either of the two products.

The FG Warehouse line shows the warehouse costs associated with carrying finished goods in inventory from one quarter to the next. In Quarter 0 no warehouse costs were charged for finished goods for either product because no inventory was carried over from last quarter.

The last line shows the sales units lost because of a lack of sufficient goods available for sale. This line also reflects the additional sales revenue you could have had during the quarter if you had sufficient goods available for sale.

Losing sales because you have an insufficient number of finished goods in stock does not just mean the loss of sales revenues for this quarter. It also creates a negative goodwill with potential customers in the next quarter. As word spreads that you do not always have the products that you advertised available, potential customers discount your advertising claims and look elsewhere to satisfy their needs. So your challenge is to keep inventories low to avoid excessive warehouse costs, while avoiding the "costs" of stocking out and having lost sales.

Labor Report

This report gives you information on the production work force used to convert raw materials into finished products. Exhibit 6.2 gives an example of this report for Quarter 0. It shows the total number of workers employed at the beginning of the quarter, plus the number of workers hired the previous quarter (i.e., the quarter before Quarter 0) that went through your training program and were capable of working this quarter. It also shows how many workers quit, were laid off, or were fired during this period of operation. The Total Available Workers shows the number of workers that were available to operate your production equipment after all these actions were considered.

Exhibit 6.2

```
UNKNOWN Industry    THRESHOLD Q 0 ACTUALS        DEMO Company 0
File  Decision  Reports  Info  Print

                        LABOR REPORT

        Labor Summary

            Beginning Workers          (#)         0
            Hired Last Quarter         (#)        45
            Current Quarter Turnover   (#)         4
            Current Quarter Layoffs    (#)         0
            Current Quarter Fired      (#)         0
            Total Available Workers    (#)        41

        Personnel Costs

            Hiring Costs               $        8000
            Layoff Costs               $           0
            Human Resource Dev.        $       10000
            Total Regular Hours        $      164000
            Overtime Premium           $           0
            Total Labor Costs          $      182000
```

This report also shows what the cost of maintaining this work force was during Quarter 0. Remember, in the quarter before Quarter 0, it cost $2,000 to hire and train and $500 to lay off a worker. The first line under Personnel Costs shows the total cost of hiring for the quarter. Appendix A shows four workers were hired in Quarter 0, so the total hiring cost was $8,000.

The remaining lines show the layoff costs, the dollars spent on employee development (i.e., the investment in Human Resource Development), regular wages, and any overtime wages you have to pay. The last line gives the total of all these costs.

Cost of Production Report

The Cost of Production Report (Exhibit 6.3) provides key information on how much it cost you to produce a finished product. This is often referred to as Manufacturing Cost of Goods Sold or Mfg COGS. This includes just the production costs, not the cost of marketing the product or financing the business. This report provides you with information regarding:
- the cost of raw materials used in the production process.
- the cost of labor used to convert raw material into finished goods.
- overhead costs associated with running the manufacturing operations.
- the cost of improvements in quality made to the product.
- depreciation charges made to reflect the aging of your plant and equipment.

Exhibit 6.3

```
UNKNOWN Industry    THRESHOLD Q 0 ACTUALS        DEMO Company 0
File  Decision  Reports  Info  Print
```

```
                    COST OF PRODUCTION REPORT

                              Prod 1      Prod 2      Totals

             Raw Material      48000       61200      109200
             Labor Costs      106537       75463      182000
             Overhead          49189       41811       91000
             Improvements      10000       17500       27500
             Depreciation      10800        9180       19980
             Total Costs      224526      205154      429680
             Production (#)     6000        5100       11100
             Unit Costs ($)    37.42       40.23       38.71

             Plant Capacity (Units)        11100
```

The costs for each element are shown for each product that you manufacture. For example, in Quarter 0 the raw material costs for Product 1 were $48,000, the labor costs were $106,537, etc. The report also shows the total for all of these costs. In Quarter 0, the total costs to manufacture Product 1 were $224,526.

You sometimes may notice that the Total Costs line does not equal the total costs of the lines being added together. This is caused by the decimal rounding performed by the program. These rounding "errors" are small (usually only a dollar or two) compared to the total costs of operating your company and are not a cause for concern. You may experience these rounding errors on any of the *Threshold* reports.

In addition to this cost information, the report also gives the per unit cost to manufacture each product. This is determined by dividing the total costs for each product by the number of units produced that quarter. For Product 1, dividing the total manufacturing costs of $224,526 by the 6,000 units produced gives the average cost per unit of $37.42.

Because the manufacturing process is fairly simple, all production of raw material into a finished product is completed at the end of each workday. This means there is no "work in process" inventory. An item in inventory is either raw material or a finished good.

It is important to recognize sources of production costs so that you can evaluate the contribution individual parts make to the total. Divide each of the individual costs for a product (e.g., raw material costs, labor costs, etc.) by the number of units of that product that were produced that quarter to get a per-unit breakdown of production costs. An example of a per-unit cost breakdown for Product 1 in Quarter 0 follows.

Exhibit 6.4

Cost Breakdown for Product 1

Source of Cost	Cost / Production Volume		Per Unit Cost	Percent
Raw Material	$ 48,000/6,000	=	$ 8.00	22.2%
Labor Costs	106,537/6,000	=	17.76	45.5%
Overhead	49,189/6,000	=	8.20	22.7%
Improvements	10,000/6,000	=	1.66	4.6%
Depreciation	10,800/6,000	=	1.80	5.0%
Total Costs	$ 224,526/6,000		$ 37.42	100.0%

Knowing how much of your per unit cost of goods sold is caused by labor costs versus material costs will help your company to better control these costs. For example, a cost breakdown could indicate whether your problems stem from poor management of your production work force or from the costs of raw materials.

The Cost of Production Report also includes the plant capacity available for production during the quarter. This shows the volume of production that you can maintain without incurring any overtime cost because your production decision exceeded plant capacity. Remember, you can also incur overtime charges if you do not have enough production workers available to handle your production volume on a regular-time basis.

SELLING AND ADMINISTRATIVE EXPENSE REPORT

This report shows the cost of advertising your two products to prospective customers. This includes the cost of television, newspaper, and magazine advertising, plus the cost of market research information you purchased this quarter. This report also shows the cost of the administrative staff in your company offices. In addition, it shows any fines assessed your company for violation of simulation rules or for charges related to dilemma decisions your company made. Finally, it also shows any refunds given to you by the simulation administrator. Exhibit 6.5 gives an example of this report for Quarter 0.

Exhibit 6.5

```
┌─ UNKNOWN Industry    THRESHOLD Q 0 ACTUALS        DEMO Company 0    ─□×─┐
│ File  Decision  Reports  Info  Print                                     │
│                                                                          │
│              SELLING AND ADMINISTRATIVE COSTS REPORT                     │
│                                                                          │
│       SELLING              Prod 1        Prod 2       Totals             │
│                                                                          │
│       TV Ads                30000         25000        55000             │
│       Newspaper Ads          9000          7000        16000             │
│       Magazine Ads          24000         21000        45000             │
│                                                                          │
│       Subtotal              63000         53000       116000             │
│                                                                          │
│       ADMINISTRATIVE                                                     │
│                                                                          │
│       Office Expense         6486          5514        12000             │
│       Market Info            5405          4595        10000             │
│       Fines                     0             0            0             │
│       Refunds                   0             0            0             │
│                                                                          │
│       TOTAL                 74892         63108       138000             │
│                                                                          │
└──────────────────────────────────────────────────────────────────────────┘
```

The total cost of sales and administration for Product 1 in Quarter 0 was $74,892. Of this total, $30,000 was spent on television advertisements, $9,000 for newspaper ads, and $24,000 for magazine ads.

The remainder of the promotional costs were administrative costs. General office expenses for staff personnel to manage your company for the quarter were $12,000. This is the cost for both of your product lines. It is split between the two products based on the sales volume of each. In Quarter 0, sales of Product 1 were 54.05% of the company's total sales (6,000/11,100 = 54.05%). Therefore, the office cost for Product 1 in Quarter 0 was 54.05% of $12,000 or $6,486. The cost for conducting market research is also split between the two products based on sales volume. This means the market research costs assigned to Product 1 in Quarter 0 were $5,405.

The operations reports (i.e., Inventory, Labor, and Cost of Production) and the Sales and Administrative Expense Report can help you assess the efficiency of your company. If you are falling short of profit goals, you need to know where the problem lies. Is the cause poor control of manufacturing costs or ineffective use of promotional dollars? By analyzing these reports, you should be able to get some sense of how to attack the problem.

INCOME STATEMENT

The purpose of the Income Statement for any quarter is to show the amount of profit or loss that occurred as a result of your company's operations that quarter. Exhibit 6.6 shows the Income Statement for *Threshold's* Quarter 0 operations. On the Income Statement, the first two lines show the sales revenue of Products 1 and 2 for the quarter. The next line gives the total sales revenues generated by the two products.

The various costs of running the business that quarter are then subtracted from the total sales revenues. The Manufacturing COGS is the first item subtracted. It is taken from the Cost of Production Report. This figure, $429,680 for Quarter 0, reflects the cost of producing finished goods that quarter. It includes depreciation charges which reflect the "wear and tear" on your plant and equipment during the production process. These costs are not cash payments made by your company, but are bookkeeping charges determined by accounting practices to show the true cost of doing business. Cash payments, alone, do not reflect all the costs of operating a business during any one period of time. For example, if you drove a car from New York City to Boston, the cost of the trip is not just the cash you paid for gasoline. You should also include such non-cash costs as tire wear and engine wear. Both of these are very real costs of your trip, even though your cash payouts for these costs would occur after your trip was completed.

Running a manufacturing process also has immediate and delayed cash payouts that are connected to its operations. You did not pay out any cash to replace plant and equipment that quarter, but you did use up some of the useful life remaining for these items. The "wear and tear" on these items needs to be reflected in your Income Statement. That way, any profit or loss shown includes all the costs of doing business.

Including these depreciation charges in the Income Statement reduces the profit you show for the quarter. This allows you to pay less tax. These tax savings can then be used to help pay for new equipment when the current equipment completely wears out. The differences between cash payments and accounting charges will be discussed in more detail under the section on the Cash Flow Statement.

Exhibit 6.6

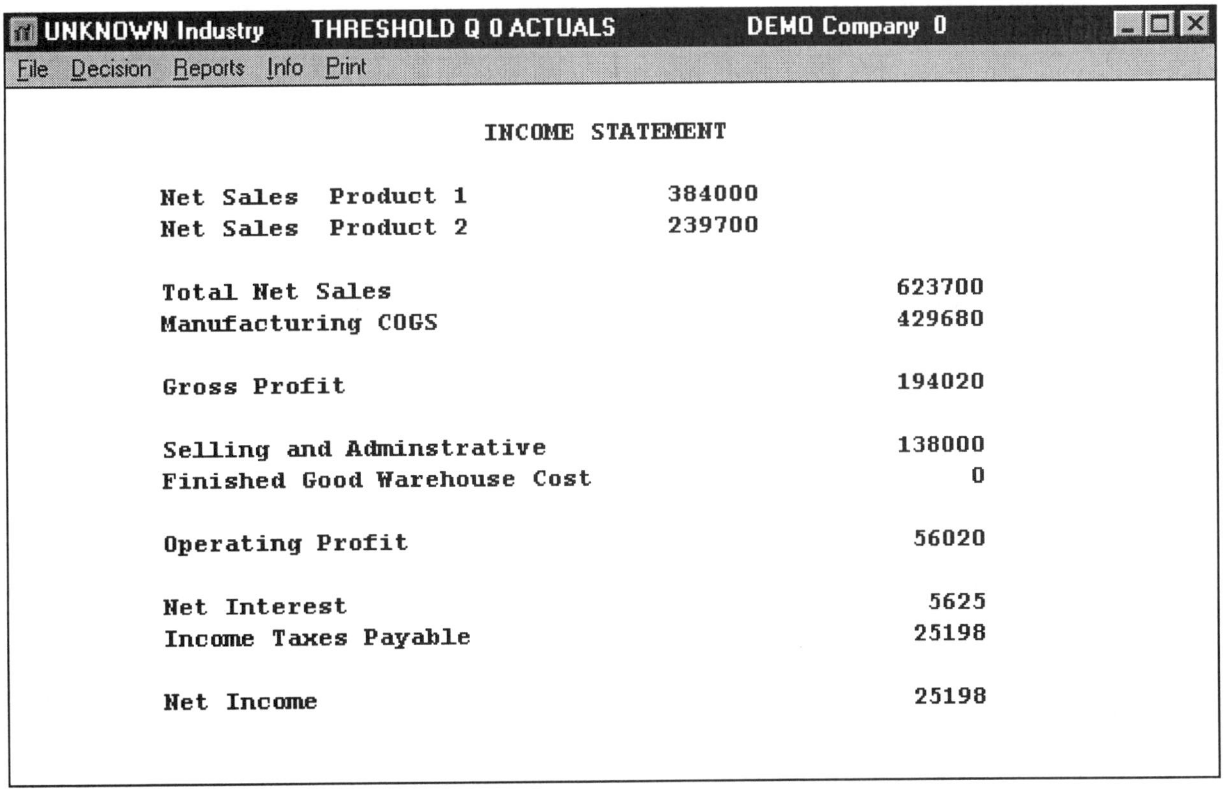

```
UNKNOWN Industry    THRESHOLD Q 0 ACTUALS         DEMO Company 0
File  Decision  Reports  Info  Print

                         INCOME STATEMENT

        Net Sales   Product 1           384000
        Net Sales   Product 2           239700

        Total Net Sales                               623700
        Manufacturing COGS                            429680

        Gross Profit                                  194020

        Selling and Adminstrative                     138000
        Finished Good Warehouse Cost                       0

        Operating Profit                               56020

        Net Interest                                    5625
        Income Taxes Payable                           25198

        Net Income                                     25198
```

The Gross Profit line shows whether your manufacturing operation generated a profit during the quarter. This is the money left after subtracting manufacturing costs (Mfg. COGS) from your sales revenues. Gross profit does not reflect all the costs of running your company because it excludes such costs as marketing and financing. It reflects just the costs of making the products and how much money your company had left after making the products. Gross profit shows the money you have left to pay for the marketing, administrative, and warehouse costs associated with running your company and promoting your products. Gross Profit was $194,020 in Quarter 0.

After deducting costs for Selling and Administrative expenses and Finished Goods Warehouse Costs, the Income Statement shows the profit resulting from operating your business. Your Operating Profits do not include the cost of financing your business. In Quarter 0, your company generated $56,020 in operating profits.

Deductions for interest payments reflect the cost of borrowing money to run the company. This includes interest for short-term loans as well as interest on any mortgages you have outstanding, less any interest income you received from your short-term investments. By keeping the costs of financing your business out of the Operating Profit calculation, you can more readily see whether problems that develop originate in how you operate your business or the financing of these operations. It is not uncommon for a business to be profitable in the making and selling of its product, but to end up losing money because it borrowed large sums to develop the business. Knowing the cause of your problem is the first step in being able to solve it.

The Income Taxes Payable line shows the taxes you must pay on any profits you earned that quarter. The current tax rate you must pay is 50%. This leaves the Net Income your company earned for the quarter. In Quarter 0, the company's Net Income was $25,198.

If you lose money in a quarter, you will not have to pay any taxes for that quarter. Further, those losses will serve as a tax shelter to counter taxes owed on profits generated in later quarters. The calculation of whether you are due any tax refunds because of losses you incurred earlier is done in the last quarter of each year. Your company's tax year started in Quarter 0 when the company began operations. Therefore, any year-end tax reconciliations will occur in Quarters 4, 8, 12, 16, etc.

BALANCE SHEET

The next report is the Balance Sheet (Exhibit 6.7). It shows the financial status of your company at the end of the quarter. The Balance Sheet is a snapshot summary indicating the Assets and Liabilities of the company at the end of that accounting period. Through it you can determine whether investments made in plant and equipment or equity investments are receiving a good rate of return.

The Balance Sheet also shows the net value (i.e., net worth) of your company. This is the liquidated value of the business if it "closed up shop" and sold everything of value to pay for everything the business owed. Whether the owners would actually collect this amount of money would depend on whether they could sell their assets for "book value" (i.e., the value of the assets shown on the Balance Sheet). The owners might end up selling the company's assets for more or less than their stated book value. This is similar to selling a used car. How much the potential buyer wants the car and what shape it is in will affect whether the car is sold at, above, or below a car dealer's "Blue Book" price. The same kind of situation holds for the seller of assets of a business. The only asset that is worth exactly what is shown on the Balance Sheet is Cash. And even this account can become open to bargaining if the company does business outside the United States and has to deal with changing rates of exchange for the dollar. This is not the case for your *Threshold* company. All your revenues are from domestic sales.

Exhibit 6.7

```
┌─────────────────────────────────────────────────────────────────────────┐
│ UNKNOWN Industry    THRESHOLD Q 0 ACTUALS        DEMO Company 0    _□×  │
│ File  Decision  Reports  Info  Print                                    │
├─────────────────────────────────────────────────────────────────────────┤
│                           BALANCE SHEET                                 │
│                                                                         │
│           ASSETS                        LIABILITIES AND OWNERS EQUITY   │
│                                                                         │
│   Current Assets                        Current Liabilities:            │
│     Cash                    49725         Short-Term Loans Payable 310000│
│     Accounts Receivable    311850         Taxes Payable             25198│
│     Investments                 0         Total Curr. Liabilities  335198│
│     Raw Material             8800                                       │
│     Finished Goods              0       Long-Term Liabilities:          │
│     Total Current Assets   370375         Mortgages Payable        240000│
│                                                                         │
│   Long-Term Assets:                       Total Liabilities        575198│
│                                                                         │
│     Plant and Equipment    499500       Owners Equity              274698│
│       Less Acc. Depreciation 19980                                      │
│     Total Long-Term Assets 479520       TOTAL LIABILITIES &        849895│
│                                         OWNERS EQUITY                   │
│   TOTAL ASSETS             849895                                       │
│                                                                         │
└─────────────────────────────────────────────────────────────────────────┘
```

Assets

The assets shown on the left side of the Balance Sheet are divided between Current Assets and Long-Term Assets. The Current Assets include cash and those assets that can be converted into cash within the next business period. (In *Threshold*, the next business period is the next quarter of operation.) Accounts Receivable shown here are different from those shown on the Cash Flow Statement (discussed in the next section). Accounts Receivable on the Balance Sheet show all the money owed by customers who have bought your product but who have not yet paid.

The other Current Assets show the value of investments you have made in short-term investments such as money market funds, and the inventories of Raw Materials and Finished Goods of the company as of the date of the Balance Sheet.

The Long-Term Assets show the original cost of the Plant and Equipment of the company and the charges that have been assessed for depreciation of those assets. Subtracting depreciation charges from the original cost of Plant and Equipment gives the current value for those assets.

Adding the Current Assets and the Long-Term Assets gives the Total Assets of the company. In Quarter 0, the Total Assets of your company were valued at $849,895.

Liabilities

The Liabilities shown on the Balance Sheet reflect the money the company owes others with which it does business. They are divided into Current Liabilities and Long-Term Liabilities.

Current Liabilities are those you will have to pay during the next quarter of business operations. These include short-term loan payments you have to make to your bank, and taxes you have to pay to the government. In Quarter 0, you owed $310,000 in short-term loans and $25,198 in taxes. Total Current Liabilities that you will have to pay in Quarter 1 are $335,198 (310,000 + 25,198).

Long-Term Liabilities on the Balance Sheet show the amount you owe the bank for mortgages you have taken out in past quarters of operations. At the end of Quarter 0, you owed $240,000 for mortgages you had taken out with your bank. Each quarter, this balance will be reduced by the quarterly payment you are required to make. The Total Liabilities account summarizes all of the money you owe to others.

Owners' Equity

Subtracting Total Liabilities from Total Assets shows the amount of equity the owners have accumulated in the business. Owners' Equity reflects what the company would be worth to the owners if the company stopped operating the business, sold off all its assets at book value and paid off all its liabilities, leaving the remainder (i.e., the Owners' Equity) for the owners of the company. At the end of Quarter 0, your company had an Owners' Equity value of $274,698. Remember, as discussed at the beginning of this section on the Balance Sheet, the owners might not collect this exact amount. Much would depend on how much the buyers of the company's assets would be willing to actually pay for them.

CASH FLOW STATEMENT

The Cash Flow Statement provides information on the cash your company received and paid out this quarter. Exhibit 6.8 shows the impact of decisions made in Quarter 0 on your company's cash flow for that quarter. Your cash receipts will typically include Cash on Hand remaining from the last quarter's operations and the Collection of Accounts Receivable. You may also periodically add to your cash receipts by requesting a Mortgage from the *Threshold* bank. The remaining cash receipts will come from money received if you decide to sell some of your plant capacity, or from any money you withdraw from your short-term investment account.

Exhibit 6.8

```
┌─ UNKNOWN Industry    THRESHOLD Q 0 ACTUALS      DEMO Company 0      _ □ ×
│ File  Decision  Reports  Info  Print
│
│                          CASH FLOW STATEMENT
│
│   CASH RECEIPTS:                      CASH PAYMENTS:
│
│      Cash on hand              0         Purchase Raw Materials    118000
│      Collection of A/R    311850         Labor and Overhead        273000
│      Mortgage                  0         Product Quality            27500
│      Sale of Plant             0         Total Warehouse Costs          0
│      ST Investment Withdrawal  0         Selling & Administrative  138000
│                                          Net Short-Term Interest        0
│   TOTAL CASH RECEIPTS     311850         Short-Term Loan Payment        0
│                                          Mortgage Interest           5625
│                                          Mortgage Retirement        10000
│   NET CASH FLOW          -260275         Income Taxes Paid              0
│   ST LOAN GRANTED         310000         Investment Deposit             0
│   NET CASH BALANCE         49725         Purchase Plant Capacity        0
│                                          TOTAL CASH PAYMENTS       572125
│
└─
```

The Cash Flow Statement differs from the Income Statement, which shows the dollar value of products you sold and the profits you earned during the quarter. The Cash Flow Statement shows the *actual* cash you received this quarter. This includes money you collected from Accounts Receivable. The Accounts Receivable on the Cash Flow Statement shows the amount of cash that was received from the accounts owing the company money for sales made in the prior quarter.

Threshold companies sell their products on credit. Normal terms are net 90 days, but some customers will pay cash for the products. For any given quarter 50% of the sales will be collected immediately, with the remaining 50% collected in the next quarter. This means the receivables from last quarter (i.e., 50% of last quarter's sales) are added to 50% of this quarter's sales to produce the cash inflow from sales for this quarter. In Quarter 0, your company collected $311,850 of your outstanding Accounts Receivable. Because of this delayed collection of sales revenues, managing your cash flow requires planning.

Having this delay between when the company sells its products and when it receives the cash for these sales is typical for almost every business. Just think of how often you pay for your purchases with a credit card. You leave the store with the merchandise and all the store has is a slip of paper that says the credit card company will send the cash later, usually months later. Yet the store owner has had to pay out *cash* for employee wages and advertising before you even entered the store. Consequently, learning how to manage your cash flow can be a key to achieving success for any organization.

Cash Payments reflect the payments your company made during the quarter. The first line under cash payments shows the payment made for raw materials received that quarter. Raw materials are paid on a cash-on-delivery basis. This means you pay for materials in the quarter you receive them, not when you order them. For example, Exhibit 6.8 shows the cash payment made for raw material purchases made before Quarter 0 began. At that time, the owners purchased 6,500 units of Product 1 raw materials worth $52,000 and 5,500 units of Product 2 raw materials worth $66,000. You received these materials in

Quarter 0 (see Inventory Reports for Quarter 0 in Appendix B) and paid the supplier $118,000 (i.e., $52,000 + $66,000).

Labor and Overhead costs are taken from the second and third lines of the Cost of Production Report. In Quarter 0 you paid a total of $182,000 in labor costs and $91,000 in overhead costs (50% of total labor costs), for a grand total of $273,000 for these two costs.

Product Quality payments shows the money spent improving the quality of your products. This figure is taken from the fourth line of the Cost of Production Report. A total of $27,500 was spent on product quality in Quarter 0.

The next line shows the total dollars spent to warehouse both the raw materials and the finished goods inventories. This cost is taken from the Inventory Report for Product 1 and Product 2. Because no raw material or finished goods inventory was carried over into Quarter 0, no costs were incurred and no payments were made.

Selling and Administrative payments are taken from the Selling & Administrative Expense Report to show the marketing and staff costs for the quarter. In Quarter 0, this totaled $138,000.

Net Short-Term Interest shows the interest payment made for money borrowed last quarter, less any interest income from short-term investments you have. If your interest income is greater than your interest expense, this number will be a minus figure to reflect the payment credit you received. The Short-Term Loan Payment line shows the amount repaid on any short-term loans you have outstanding. No short-term loans were requested last quarter, so no short-term loan or interest payments were due in Quarter 0.

The Mortgage Interest line shows the interest paid on mortgages the bank has issued your company. In Quarter 0 you paid $5,625 in Mortgage Interest. Payments to retire (i.e., pay off) your mortgages are shown on the following line. You are presently paying $10,000 per quarter on the mortgage you have with the *Threshold* bank.

The Income Taxes Paid line shows the taxes you had to pay out. This is different from Income Taxes Payable on the Income Statement because those are not paid out in cash until the next quarter of operation. For Quarter 0 no taxes were paid on Quarter 0 profits because they are not due until Quarter 1.

The Investments Deposit line shows any investments you made in short-term money markets this quarter. No short-term investments were made in Quarter 0.

The last cash payment line shows payments you made to purchase additional plant capacity. *Threshold* requires that all plant capacity purchases be paid in cash the day that the capacity is ready for use. Any plant purchased this quarter is not usable until next quarter and payment for it is due next quarter. This payment schedule means you do not have to arrange financing for the purchase of plant capacity until the quarter following the purchase. Remember, you receive any money you borrow the same quarter you request it.

The last line shows the total of the Cash Payments made that quarter. In Quarter 0 this totaled $572,125.

The last three lines on the left side of the Cash Flow Statement are Net Cash Flow, Short-Term Loan Granted, and Net Cash Balance. Net Cash Flow is the result of subtracting Total Cash Payments from Cash Receipts. Net Cash Flow reflects the cash generated by this quarter's operations or, if a minus figure, the cash needed to finance the operations. If you need a short-term loan to cover a cash shortfall, you must be sure to determine accurately the amount of your cash needs and request that amount. *Threshold* places a premium on cash planning and forecasting. Any time your company does not have a zero or positive cash balance, you will receive an automatic emergency loan from your bank to bring your cash balance up to zero. The interest rate for an emergency loan will be double the normal rate for short-term loans.

This emergency loan will be at higher than normal interest rates to cover the cost of making the loan on such short notice. Remember, as explained in Chapter 5 under the Short-Term Loans section, the *Threshold* bank charges you this higher interest on the total loan granted, not just on the difference between the amount you requested and amount actually needed. The Net Cash Balance shows the total of your Net Cash Flow and Short-Term Loan. If your Net Cash Balance is zero, it probably means you did not request a short-term loan large enough to cover all your cash needs for the quarter. Either that, or you were incredibly lucky and had requested the precise amount of cash you needed when you turned in your disk for processing by your instructor. Remember, as was discussed in Chapter 5, you need to request a short term loan that balances the risk of falling short of actual cash needs and incurring an emergency loan, with the expense of paying interest charges on money not really needed.

INDUSTRY PERFORMANCE REPORT

In addition to reports on the performance of your individual company, you will also receive two industry performance reports. Both reports will provide you with information for all companies in your *Threshold* industry on four factors: sales, income, return on assets (ROA), and the accuracy of each company's sales forecasts. One of the industry performance reports shows the performance of all the companies on these four factors for the current quarter. The other report shows a game-to-date summary on these factors. Appendix H provides an example of both of these reports.

Exhibit 6.9 shows an example of just the Quarter Performance Report. We will use this example to discuss each of the four performance factors and explain how the *Threshold* program calculates the points assigned to each team in the PTS AWRD columns.

Exhibit 6.9

```
EXAMPLE Industry    THRESHOLD Q 3 ACTUALS           DEMO 1 Company 1
File  Decision  Reports  Info  Print

                    QUARTER PERFORMANCE REPORT

              PTS            PTS            PTS    FORECAST  PTS   OVERALL
COMP  SALES   AWRD  INCOME   AWRD   ROA     AWRD   ERRORS    AWRD  PTS  RANK
  1.  604389   8    18240    30     1.92    17     1270      10*   65    3
  2.  704704  10*   30700    50*    3.40    30*    1762       7    97    1
  3.  715600  10*   20731    34     2.24    20     3706       3    67    2
```

For each of the four factors, the report shows each company's performance, plus a ranking and evaluation of that performance. The column under each heading -- Sales, Income, etc. -- shows what each company achieved for that factor in that quarter. Figures shown for the sales, income, and return on assets factors, indicate each company's actual performance. For example, Company 3 had sales revenues for Quarter 3 of $715,600 and net income of $20,731. Both of these figures are taken from the company's Income Statement for the quarter. Company 3's ROA (i.e., return on assets) was 2.24, which indicates the company's net income represents a 2.24% return on the total assets of the company, as listed on its Balance Sheet. To calculate your company's ROA, divide your net income by the total assets of your company.

For the sales forecast factor, the figure shows the *absolute* difference in unit sales between the *actual demand* generated by a company's marketing efforts and the sales *forecast* made by that company. The report does not make any distinction on whether the sales forecast was high or low. It is only concerned with how inaccurate the forecast was from the actual demand generated for a company's products. Notice that it is actual demand, not actual sales, that is used to determine this factor. This means any sales lost due to stockouts will be included in determining the accuracy of a company's sales forecasting. For this factor the smallest error indicates the best performance. In Exhibit 6.9, Company 3 had combined total unit sales forecast errors for both products of 3,706 for Quarter 3.

The Points Awarded (Pts Awrd) columns show the number of points awarded based on each company's performance on the four factors. The points awarded to each company for their performance on a particular factor are calculated based on (a) that company's performance relative to the company that achieved the best performance on that factor and (b) the maximum possible points that could be achieved for that factor. For example, Exhibit 6.9 shows that the points awarded Company 3 for the Net Income factor were 34. This was calculated by dividing Company 3's income for the quarter by Company 2's quarterly income and then multiplying that by 50 ([20,731/30,700] * 50). In this example, Company 3's income was 67.5% (20,731/30,700) of the company which achieved the best income for the quarter (Company 2). Consequently, Company 3 received 67.5% of the maximum possible points (50) that could be achieved for that factor. This resulted in a Pts Awrd of 34 (67.5% * 50). In our example, Company 3 was awarded a total of 67 points for its performance in Quarter 3. It received 10 points for sales revenues, 34 points for income, 20 points for its ROA, and 3 points for its forecasting errors. This performance earned Company 3 a ranking of number 2 in the industry for that quarter.

As with the Quarter Performance Report, the Game-to-Date summary shows the total points awarded to a company based on the number of points it received on each of the four performance factors. For the Game-to-Date report, these calculations are based on all quarters of operation. For the sales, net income, and sales forecast factors, the Game-to-Date report is an *accumulation* of the combined total of all quarters of operation. For the ROA factor, this report shows the *average* for all quarters of operation, rather than the total of the quarters. This allows a better comparison of game-to-date performance with current-quarter performance. The Game-to-Date summary also shows the rank of each company based on the total points it had been awarded.

The maximum possible points for a factor are determined for each of the four factors by the instructor. By doing this, the instructor indicates the relative importance of each of the factors. The points allocated to each factor can range from 0 to 100, but the total of all points allocated for the four factors must equal exactly 100. This means if one factor is allocated 100 points, all other factors would have to be allocated 0 points. Usually at least a few points are allocated to each factor.

You should now have a basic understanding of each of the *Threshold* reports that you will work with throughout the simulation exercise. The more you work with them, the greater your confidence should become in using them to manage your company. While these reports are simplistic compared to those of large, complex organizations, the principles for using the reports to gain insight into how to manage any company are similar. Learning how to analyze where your costs are coming from, and how to control these costs, is a key to working within any company. We hope and believe the challenges you face in this simulation experience will aid you in that process.

Good luck.

APPENDIXES

APPENDIX A

```
UNKNOWN Industry    THRESHOLD Q 0 ACTUALS         DEMO Company 0
File  Decision  Reports  Info  Print
```

MARKETING DECISION REPORT

		Product 1	Product 2
Price	($)	64	47
TV Ads	(Minutes)	6	5
Newspaper (Column Inches)		9	7
Magazine Ads	(Pages)	8	7
Sales Forecast	(Units)	6000	5100
Actual Demand	(Units)	6000	5100

MARKETING RESEARCH DECISION REPORT

Price	N	Product Quality	N
TV Ads	N	Units Sold	N
Newspaper Ads	N	Future Sales Potential (Qtr)	1
Magazine Ads	N		

```
UNKNOWN Industry    THRESHOLD Q 0 ACTUALS         DEMO Company 0
File  Decision  Reports  Info  Print
```

PRODUCTION DECISION REPORT

	Product 1	Product 2
Buy Raw Materials (#)	7000	6500
Invest in Product Quality	10000	17500
Units Produced (#)	6000	5100

Workers:	Hire	4	Fire	0	Layoff	0
Plant Capacity:	Buy	0	Sell	0		
Human Resource Development		10000				

FINANCE DECISION REPORT

Short-Term Loan:	Request	310000	S T Investment: Deposit	0
Mortgage:	Request	0	Withdrawal	0
	Extra Payment	0		

NO DILEMMA DECISION THIS QUARTER

APPENDIX B

QUARTER 0 REPORTS

```
UNKNOWN Industry    THRESHOLD Q 0 ACTUALS         DEMO Company 0
File Decision Reports Info Print
```

	Product 1		Product 2	
RAW MATERIAL INVENTORY REPORT	Units	Value	Units	Value
Beginning Balance	0	0	0	0
Units Received	6500	52000	5500	66000
Total Available	6500	52000	5500	66000
Used in Production	6000	48000	5100	61200
Ending Balance	500	4000	400	4800
Raw Matl Warehouse Costs	0	0	0	0
Total Product Cost		48000		61200

	Product 1			Product 2		
FINISHED GOODS INVENTORY REPORT	Units	$/Unit	Value	Units	$/Unit	Value
Beginning Balance	0	.00	0	0	.00	0
Production	6000	37.42	224526	5100	40.23	205154
Units to Sell	6000	37.42	224526	5100	40.23	205154
Units Sold	6000	37.42	224526	5100	40.23	205154
End Balance	0	.00	0	0	.00	0
FG Warehouse	0	2.50	0	0	1.50	0
Lost Sales	0	64.00	0	0	47.00	0

```
UNKNOWN Industry    THRESHOLD Q 0 ACTUALS         DEMO Company 0
File Decision Reports Info Print
```

LABOR REPORT

Labor Summary

Beginning Workers	(#)	0
Hired Last Quarter	(#)	45
Current Quarter Turnover	(#)	4
Current Quarter Layoffs	(#)	0
Current Quarter Fired	(#)	0
Total Available Workers	(#)	41

Personnel Costs

Hiring Costs	$	8000
Layoff Costs	$	0
Human Resource Dev.	$	10000
Total Regular Hours	$	164000
Overtime Premium	$	0
Total Labor Costs	$	182000

COST OF PRODUCTION REPORT

	Prod 1	Prod 2	Totals
Raw Material	48000	61200	109200
Labor Costs	106537	75463	182000
Overhead	49189	41811	91000
Improvements	10000	17500	27500
Depreciation	10800	9180	19980
Total Costs	224526	205154	429680
Production (#)	6000	5100	11100
Unit Costs ($)	37.42	40.23	38.71
Plant Capacity (Units)		11100	

SELLING AND ADMINISTRATIVE COSTS REPORT

SELLING	Prod 1	Prod 2	Totals
TV Ads	30000	25000	55000
Newspaper Ads	9000	7000	16000
Magazine Ads	24000	21000	45000
Subtotal	63000	53000	116000
ADMINISTRATIVE			
Office Expense	6486	5514	12000
Market Info	5405	4595	10000
Fines	0	0	0
Refunds	0	0	0
TOTAL	74892	63108	138000

Appendix B, Quarter 0 Reports 77

```
UNKNOWN Industry    THRESHOLD Q 0 ACTUALS    DEMO Company 0
File  Decision  Reports  Info  Print
```

INCOME STATEMENT

Net Sales Product 1	384000	
Net Sales Product 2	239700	
Total Net Sales		623700
Manufacturing COGS		429680
Gross Profit		194020
Selling and Adminstrative		138000
Finished Good Warehouse Cost		0
Operating Profit		56020
Net Interest		5625
Income Taxes Payable		25198
Net Income		25198

```
UNKNOWN Industry    THRESHOLD Q 0 ACTUALS    DEMO Company 0
File  Decision  Reports  Info  Print
```

BALANCE SHEET

ASSETS		LIABILITIES AND OWNERS EQUITY	
Current Assets		Current Liabilities:	
Cash	49725	Short-Term Loans Payable	310000
Accounts Receivable	311850	Taxes Payable	25198
Investments	0	Total Curr. Liabilities	335198
Raw Material	8800		
Finished Goods	0	Long-Term Liabilities:	
Total Current Assets	370375	Mortgages Payable	240000
Long-Term Assets:		Total Liabilities	575198
Plant and Equipment	499500	Owners Equity	274698
Less Acc. Depreciation	19980		
Total Long-Term Assets	479520	TOTAL LIABILITIES &	849895
		OWNERS EQUITY	
TOTAL ASSETS	849895		

CASH FLOW STATEMENT

CASH RECEIPTS:		CASH PAYMENTS:	
Cash on hand	0	Purchase Raw Materials	118000
Collection of A/R	311850	Labor and Overhead	273000
Mortgage	0	Product Quality	27500
Sale of Plant	0	Total Warehouse Costs	0
ST Investment Withdrawal	0	Selling & Administrative	138000
		Net Short-Term Interest	0
TOTAL CASH RECEIPTS	311850	Short-Term Loan Payment	0
		Mortgage Interest	5625
		Mortgage Retirement	10000
NET CASH FLOW	-260275	Income Taxes Paid	0
ST LOAN GRANTED	310000	Investment Deposit	0
NET CASH BALANCE	49725	Purchase Plant Capacity	0
		TOTAL CASH PAYMENTS	572125

COST PARAMETERS REPORT

	Product 1	Product 2
Raw Material	8.00	12.00
Raw Material Warehouse	1.00	2.00
Finished Goods Warehouse	2.50	1.50
Worker Productivity	250	300

Television Ad Minutes	$ 5000	Mkt Research-Product Price	$	5000
Newspaper Ad Column Inches	$ 1000	Mkt Research-TV ADs Minutes	$	5000
Magazine Ad Pages	$ 3000	Mkt Research-Newspaper Ads	$	3000
Workers' Quarterly Wages	$ 4000	Mkt Research-Magazine Ads	$	4000
Hiring Costs per Worker	$ 2000	Mkt Research-Product Quality	$	2000
Layoff Costs per Worker	$ 500	Mkt Research-Unit Sales	$	5000
Administrative Expenses	$ 12000	Mkt Research-Market Demand	$	10000
New Plant Cost per Unit	$ 45	Manufacturing Overhead Rate	%	50.0
Short-Term Loan Rate	% 10.0	Mortgage Interest Rate	%	9.0
Short-Term Investment Rate	% 5.0			

APPENDIX C

SAMPLE MARKET RESEARCH REPORT
FOR A THREE-TEAM INDUSTRY

```
     EXAMPLE Industry    THRESHOLD Q 3 ACTUALS        DEMO 1 Company 1
 File  Decision  Reports  Info  Print

                          MARKETING RESEARCH
Co      PRICE      TV ADS       NEWS       MAG       QUALITY      UNITS SOLD
 #    P1   P2     P1   P2     P1   P2    P1   P2    P1      P2     P1     P2

1.    69   58      4    3      7    5    10   12   15000   22000   4727   4797
2.    66   55      6    5      9    7     8    7   10000   17500   6594   4900
3.    64   54     10    7     12    8     3    1    8000   15000   6733   5272

    Potential product demands for Quarter 6 are 7300 and 6000 respectively.
```

APPENDIX D

INITIAL COST PARAMETERS

```
UNKNOWN Industry    THRESHOLD Q 0 ACTUALS         DEMO Company 0
File Decision Reports Info Print

                      COST PARAMETERS REPORT

                                      Product 1    Product 2

           Raw Material                  8.00        12.00
           Raw Material Warehouse        1.00         2.00
           Finished Goods Warehouse      2.50         1.50
           Worker Productivity            250          300

Television Ad Minutes       $   5000   Mkt Research-Product Price     $   5000
Newspaper Ad Column Inches  $   1000   Mkt Research-TV ADs Minutes    $   5000
Magazine Ad Pages           $   3000   Mkt Research-Newspaper Ads     $   3000
Workers' Quarterly Wages    $   4000   Mkt Research-Magazine Ads      $   4000
Hiring Costs per Worker     $   2000   Mkt Research-Product Quality   $   2000
Layoff Costs per Worker     $    500   Mkt Research-Unit Sales        $   5000
Administrative Expenses     $  12000   Mkt Research-Market Demand     $  10000
New Plant Cost per Unit     $     45   Manufacturing Overhead Rate    %   50.0
Short-Term Loan Rate        %   10.0   Mortgage Interest Rate         %    9.0
Short-Term Investment Rate  %    5.0
```

EXHIBIT E

THRESHOLD LIMITS AND TIME LAGS

```
THRESHOLD LIMITS AND TIME LAGS
       MARKETING AND FINANCE
```

Decision Variable		Range/ Limits	Lag Before Impact
Product Decisions – Product 1 and Product 2			
Price	($)	0 – 99	Immediate
TV Ads	(Minutes)	0 – 99	Immediate
Newspaper Ads	(Column Inches)	0 – 99	Immediate
Magazine Ads	(Pages)	0 – 99	Immediate
Product Quality	($)	0 – 99999	Immediate
Sales Forecast – Product 1 & 2	(#)	0 – 99999	No Impact
Short-Term Loan Requested	($)	0 – 9999999	Immediate
Mortgage Request	($)	0 – 9999999	Immediate
Short-Term Investment	($)	0 – 999999	Immediate
Short-Term Withdrawal	($)	0 – 999999	Immediate
Extra Payment	($)	0 – 999999	Immediate

```
THRESHOLD LIMITS AND TIME LAGS
           PRODUCTION
```

Decision Variable		Range/ Limits	Lag Before Impact
Human Resource Development	($)	0 – 99999	1 Quarter
Workers Hired for Next Quarter	(#)	0 – 99	1 Quarter
Workers Fired This Quarter	(#)	0 – 99	Immediate
Workers Laid Off This Quarter	(#)	0 – 99	Immediate
Purchase Plant Capacity	(# of Units)	0 – 40000	1 Quarter
(Maximum of 50% of current capacity)			
Sell Plant Capacity	(# of Units)	0 – 40000	1 Quarter
(Maximum of 50% of current capacity)			
Product 1 or Product 2:			
Purchase Raw Material	(#)	0 – 99999	1 Quarter
Production Volume	(#)	0 – 99999	Immediate

APPENDIX F

THRESHOLD "HOT" KEYS

Screen	"Hot" Key(s)
To see	Press

Decisions
Marketing & Market Research	F1
Production & Finance	F2

Reports
Marketing Decisions	CTRL + F1
Production Decisions	CTRL + F2
Inventory	CTRL + V
Labor	CTRL + L
Production Costs	CTRL + P
Selling/Administration	CTRL + S
Income Statement	CTRL + I
Balance Sheet	CTRL + B
Cash Flow	CTRL + C
Market Research	CTRL + R
Quarter Performance	CTRL + Q
Game-to-Date Performance	CTRL + G

Info
Marketing Limits	SHIFT + F1
Production Limits	SHIFT + F2
Costs	F3
Bulletin	F4

Appendix G

Management Dilemmas

MANAGEMENT DILEMMA 1
WHY DOES IT HAVE TO BE EMILY?

"... and whichever of the decisions you choose to make on this matter is totally up to you." The door closes behind you as you walk out of David Anderscott's office. Just what you need, another smoldering fire that might burst into flames no matter what you do. You stop and chat with several office workers on your way back to your office. But your mind is really on this new situation concerning Emily Bergmeier.

Emily is your purchasing agent and has been a trusted employee in Anderscott organizations for many years. She has a business degree from one of the better schools and has used her knowledge to keep your total purchasing expenditures among the lowest in the industry. Anderscott has just informed you that Emily has been accepting payments from one of your suppliers. For every $100 of goods she buys from the supplier, she receives a payment of $1 in the form of merchandise or cash mailed to her home. Information obtained by Anderscott indicates that no cost to the company can be traced to her actions. In fact, her performance has made her a highly recruited professional.

You must decide what to do about this embarrassing, if not illegal, situation. Your options, as spelled out by Anderscott are to:

1. Do nothing since Emily is performing well and your costs are among the lowest in the industry.

    The effect of this action could result in a $25,000 fine by industry governmental regulators. If you are fined, it will be paid next quarter.

2. Terminate Emily immediately. Call the supplier and tell them of the problem. Inform your new purchasing agent not to purchase from that supplier in the future.

    The effect of this action could cause raw material costs to increase by 40% next quarter.

3. Terminate Emily immediately. Call the supplier and tell them of the problem. Inform your new purchasing agent not to accept payments from any of your suppliers.

    The effect of this action could cause raw material costs to increase by 25% next quarter.

4. Discipline Emily immediately. Call the supplier and tell them of the problem. Inform Emily not to accept payments from the supplier.

    The effect of this action could cause raw material costs to increase by 10% next quarter.

5. Appoint a committee of supervisors to investigate the accusations and report back to you with their findings and recommendations.

    The effect of this action could result in a $20,000 fine by industry governmental regulators if no corrective action seems likely. You would pay this fine next quarter.

Enter the number of your decision on the Production and Finance screen.

MANAGEMENT DILEMMA 2
CAN YOU STEAL GARBAGE?

Glancing up at the clock you realize that it's almost 11:30 p.m. You put away the papers you've been working on, pick up your coat, and walk out of your office into the empty plant. A flash of light catches your eye as you look down the alleyway lined with company trash carts. You see the outline of a pickup truck and a person loading items into the back of it. Strange, you think as you walk over and turn on the alley lights, no one should be here at this time. You see one of your production workers, Miles Molbeck.

"Hey, Miles!" you call. "What's going on here?"

"Uh, oh ... Hello, boss. What brings you here at this hour?" Miles asks you as you continue to walk closer.

"I haven't been home yet," you say, "but what are you doing here? You know the plant is off-limits after working hours."

"Oh... uh... I'm just here collecting these corrugated cartons that contained our raw materials. You know my wife's been sick and I need a few extra bucks. I learned a high-school buddy uses discarded corrugated paper in his business, and he pays seventy cents for a hundred pounds of crushed boxes. I take these home, smash them, and then sell them to him. I'm not getting rich on it. It just helps pay the bills. Anyway, this is garbage. It's not of any value to the company. In fact, you pay to have it hauled away, don't you?"

"That's not the issue," you say. "You know the company policy on theft. Anyone caught stealing company property is subject to immediate discharge and criminal prosecution. Those boxes are company property, and you have no authority to take them. That constitutes theft. Unload those boxes and go home. I want you in my office at nine o'clock tomorrow morning. Now get out of here."

"Yeah, sure. What a rinky-dink outfit. I'm going to be fired for stealing garbage that you're paying to have hauled away to the landfill."

Great, you think. What am I going to do now? You sympathize with Miles, and deep down agree that theft of garbage is a silly charge. But the company policy on theft is very specific and you must be wary of setting a precedent that goes against it. Can you really look the other way? Is Miles any different from any other employee? What if someone else needs money? Is it fair to the other employees? Who determines what is and what isn't garbage?

On the other hand, what happens if you fire Miles? Is employee morale going to be lowered? What about public opinion? Miles is well liked by the workers and popular in the community. Will business suffer because of bad press?

Your options are to:

1. Do nothing.

    If you choose this course of action, employee morale reaction is uncertain. Some of the employees will applaud your actions as humanitarian, while other employees who may also be in financial straits will feel slighted. This could have an affect on worker productivity. Also of concern is that you don't know what Anderscott will say if he ever hears about the incident.

2. Fire Miles and prosecute him for theft.

    This action will ensure that you have no extraordinary losses because of theft. But this action will probably lower productivity for several quarters.

3. Discipline Miles by suspending him for one quarter without pay.

    You anticipate this action will prevent losses because of theft, but employee morale will probably suffer. Thus you expect an increase in production costs for several quarters.

4. Subject Miles to minor discipline and a reprimand.

    Little effect on morale is anticipated. However, the minor punishment may encourage other employees to steal. This action might cause an increase in losses of up to $20,000 next quarter.

Enter the number of your decision on the Production and Finance screen.

MANAGEMENT DILEMMA 3
THE OLDER EMPLOYEE

One of your employees in the Marketing Department has not been able to adequately perform his assigned duties. He is a long-standing employee who has been with the company for 19 years. While he was an able employee in the past, the changing demands of the business, along with expanding job requirements for his position, have resulted in performance that is severely lacking. He is 57 years old. In one more year he will receive extra retirement benefits granted to 20-year employees. If you continue to "carry him" (employ him) for that year, you will undoubtedly have to hire an extra employee to "pick up the slack." This could also set a precedent for other employees facing similar circumstances throughout the company. On the other hand, firing him could effect the morale and loyalty of other employees. You also worry that if you fire him he will sue claiming age discrimination. Your assessment of the situation leads you to the following options with the following consequences.

1. Carry the employee for 1 year until his retirement benefits are in full force.

    This would necessitate hiring an additional employee to perform many of the duties this employee should be performing, but is not able to handle. The full cost of this employee (i.e., wages, benefits, office space, etc.) would be $40,000. The owners have said you would have to set aside $40,000 next quarter to pay for this action.

    There is a debate among your legal advisors whether this sets a precedence that would require similar treatment of other "older" employees. If similar treatment is required, you will have to pay an additional $50,000 into an escrow account next quarter.

2. Fire the employee.

    This will cost your company $27,000 as a severance payment to the employee (one half of one year's salary). This will be paid next quarter.

    If a lawsuit is filed, company lawyers estimate the total cost, regardless of who wins the suit, to be $100,000. These costs would be paid next quarter.

3. Offer the employee early retirement with full benefits of a 20-year employee.

    This will cost the company an additional (i.e., beyond current retirement benefit costs) $50,000 in retirement benefits costs. This would be paid into an escrow account next quarter. You know the employee prefers to continue to work until he is 62 years old. Even with the benefits offered, his annual income will drop considerably.

    If other "older" employees demand equal treatment, you estimate the company would have to pay an additional $50,000 into its retirement fund to pay for these costs. This payment would be made next quarter. Your Human Resource people think there is little chance of this demand for equal treatment occurring.

4. Spend an additional $65,000 in training for a special program to improve the productivity of your older workers.

    The $65,000 must be paid next quarter. Your Human Resources people believe the productivity of the older workers would be improved to a level so that no additional action would have to be taken.

Enter the number of your decision on the Production and Finance screen.

MANAGEMENT DILEMMA 4
THE ALCOHOLIC EMPLOYEE

One of your employees has returned from lunch in various stages of drunkenness many times over the past three weeks. Without question, his drinking affects his performance as well as that of those around him. You are concerned that this could be a problem throughout the company. Rather than treat this as an isolated case concerning one employee, you are considering the possibility of instituting company-wide policies and programs.

Your options are to:

1. Do nothing and hope things get better.

    There is no direct cost to this, but other workers may get upset having to work with this person and quit. There is also the chance this worker could be injured on the job because of the effects of the intoxication. Your liability because of your inaction could cost you up to $20,000.

2. Require the employee to attend a chemical-abuse program.

    This is a residence program that lasts for three months. You will pay the employee's salary while he is on leave, plus the cost of the program. The total cost will be $10,000.

    If he refuses to attend, he will be terminated. The costs associated with this would be $3,000. If he attends the program, but quits before its completion, the cost would be $15,000.

3. Institute a company-wide Chemical Abuse Awareness Program.

    The cost of this program would be $24,000. Your expectation is that productivity would be improved. This would mean higher crew productivity on the shop floor. The extent of these gains is unpredictable given the lack of experience the company has with this type of program. While only temporary, your Human Resources manager estimates it could range anywhere from 3 to 8%.

4. Put the employee on notice that repeating this behavior will result in termination.

    There is no cost if the employee mends his ways. Termination costs will be $3,000 if he comes in drunk again. Chances are this is likely to occur. Other workers may react negatively to your lack of a positive approach.

Enter the number of your decision on the Production and Finance screen.

MANAGEMENT DILEMMA 5
WILDCAT STRIKE

A small group of your production employees are dissatisfied with the shop rules. They are also upset with their pay levels given the prevailing wage rates in their community for their type of work. In addition, they claim their fringe-benefit package is inadequate. They have been promoting the idea of a wildcat strike among the rest of the production workers as a means to get immediate attention to their concerns rather than wait for the current contract to expire. It is unlikely that the whole production workforce would join in a strike, but a significant portion could. Conceding to some or all of their demands would effect the chances of a strike occurring, but could also have an impact on future contract negotiations.

Your options are to:

1. Do nothing and hope that calmer heads on the shop floor will prevail.

    If a strike occurs it could mean up to 20% of your production workers could walk out this quarter. It would take the union leadership one quarter to get the workers to return to their jobs.

2. Offer a bonus of $10,000 as recognition of the legitimacy of their concerns.

    This would significantly reduce the chance of a strike occurring, but not guarantee it.

3. Offer a bonus that would cost a total of $20,000.

    This would make the likelihood of a strike small.

4. Offer a bonus that would cost a total of $50,000.

    No strike would occur.

5. Fire the workers involved.

    Chances of a walk-out for one quarter by 25% of the production workforce would be 50 - 50.

Enter the number of your decision on the Production and Finance screen.

MANAGEMENT DILEMMA 6
THE SUBSTITUTE RAW MATERIALS

You have a chance to acquire a supply of substitute raw materials for Product #1. A large salvage company is accepting closed bids for a type of plastic slightly different from the raw material you presently use. A materials consultant thinks that this material would be an adequate substitute. Nothing appeared wrong with the sample material he inspected. Your production manager, Sylvia Wainright is concerned that not all the material would meet your quality standards. She estimates that up to 30% of the material might not be usable. She also believes that your bid will affect the quality of the raw materials you receive. The higher the bid, the higher the quality of the materials received.

The salvage company has decided to sell the materials in lot sizes of 20,000 units. It will not sell more than one lot of 20,000 to any one company.

Since this is a closed bid, you will not know how much others are bidding for the materials. You will be allowed to make only one bid. How much you bid will affect the likelihood of successfully getting the material.

Anderscott has authorized you to make a bid on these materials, if you choose to do so. However, he has made it clear that the decision on whether to make a bid, or how much to bid, is yours to make. If you bid for the materials, and win, the number of units you will receive will be *in addition to* whatever volume purchase from your regular supplier.

Your options are to:

1. Make no bid.

2. Make a bid of 50% of the current price you are paying for raw materials for Product #1.

3. Make a bid of 65% of the current price you are paying for raw materials for Product #1.

4. Make a bid of 80% of the current price you are paying for raw materials for Product #1.

Enter the number of your decision on the Production and Finance screen.

MANAGEMENT DILEMMA 7
WHERE THERE'S SMOKE, THERE'S FIRE

"Remember," says Anderscott, "the new policy is your baby. We're not required to have a smoking policy in this state, but a 1988 survey conducted by the U. S. Department of Health showed 35.6% of the companies in their survey had an employee help program concerning tobacco. The program will cost us money, but the benefits should outweigh the costs. Let me know what you decide to do."

The next day you meet with various employees and talk with other managers you know. After considerable discussion, you identify the following smoking policy alternatives.

Your options are to:

1. Do nothing beyond providing no-smoking sections in the eating areas.

    There are no data that show your firm incurs any costs caused by tobacco. You believe employees should make their own decisions regarding smoking and its health effects.

    There is the chance that non-smokers will complain to the Health Department about second-hand smoke throughout the company buildings. Costs associated with responding to the Health Department inquiries and tests could cost up to $30,000.

2. Adopt a "smoke free" policy that prohibits tobacco use in the building and on company property.

    The administration costs of the policy are expected to be $20,000 and will be paid into an escrow account this quarter. You estimate that productivity might increase by up to 4% because of a reduction in sick leave taken.

    You anticipate some resistance since almost 20% of your workforce smoke. The increased level of discontent and problems associated with nicotine withdrawal could negate any productivity gains.

3. Adopt a "smoke free" environment in the buildings but allow tobacco use outside and in personal vehicles on the company parking lot.

    The cost of this program is $15,000 with payment into an escrow account this quarter. You estimate that this program may increase productivity by 2%.

    You expect little direct opposition to this program from the workforce but predict the policy will increase the length of coffee breaks and lunches taken by smokers in your company. Non-smokers are likely to extend their break periods as well.

4. Create a "smoking lounge" where tobacco use is allowed and permit tobacco use outside all buildings.

    The smoking lounge will have special fans and trash receptacles that cost $5,000. This will bring the total cost of the lounge to $8,000 with payment into an escrow account this quarter.

    You expect no resistance from the workforce, but extra trips to the tobacco lounge could cause a slight drop in productivity.

5. Put up No Smoking signs in the plant, require smokers to sit in a special area in the canteen, and prohibit smoking in all open offices.

   The cost of this policy is $5,000 with payment into an escrow account this quarter. You expect little worker dissent and benefits will be minimal.

   There is a possibility that non-smokers may complain to the Health Department about second-hand smoke in the canteen. The costs associated with responding to the Health Department inquiries and tests could cost up to $10,000.

Enter the number of your decision on the Production and Finance screen.

MANAGEMENT DILEMMA 8
DID YOU HEAR THE ONE ABOUT . . . ?

Lee, your personnel director, is in the process of giving you some disturbing information. You asked her to look into why the turnover for the administrative office staff in your organization is three times the industry average. You initially thought the high turnover rate was because the positions are entry-level, minimum-wage, and clerical. You asked Lee look into the issue and report back to you. She conducted a number of interviews with the staff as well as exit interviews with individuals who quit during the last month.

". . . and I think the exit interview with Rebecca Meeker confirms my diagnosis," says Lee. "We have two employees in the plant whose actions people in administration find unpleasant. Our warehouse coordinator, Butch Pilson, and a clerk in receiving named Tom West are the culprits. They tell off-color stories and jokingly proposition *every* woman in the office, regardless of how attractive the woman is."

"Many see the behavior as harmless bantering, but I think Rebecca's right. Butch and Tom's behavior borders on sexual harassment. Rebecca says she is considering a lawsuit, and there is the chance of a judgment against us. Glad this is your problem to solve."

You look back and see that no one has ever complained about the two men officially before this. Butch and Tom are among your best and most well-liked employees. Most of the employees seem to enjoy the verbal dueling. They accept it in the spirit of fun, not as serious attempts to proposition the women or degrade them.

Still, you cannot ignore the facts. Turnover in one department is three times the industry average. On top of all this, the threat of a sexual harassment lawsuit now hangs over your head. If a lawsuit is filed, you estimate legal costs would be $10,000 even if you won, and five times that if you lost the case. After much thought, you identify the following alternatives.

Your options are to:

1. Do nothing.

    You feel the evidence you have is not conclusive enough to take any action. If you accuse the individuals of sexual harassment, you might ruin their careers. Without hard proof, the two men could sue the company for defamation of character. But how would the women react to this lack of action on your part?

    You anticipate no direct costs with this action. However, the turnover problem would continue and there would be a relatively large probability of legal action. If a suit is filed, you will almost certainly lose because you took no action to stop the men's behavior.

2. Fire Butch and Tom.

   You feel that a warning would only create a division among employees as each chose a side. Taking a firm stand would reinforce the company's attitude on behavior such as this.

   A cost of $15,000 would be incurred to cover severance pay and pension donations for the two individuals. This action virtually guarantees no legal action will be taken against your company for sexual harassment.

   You expect there is little chance either of the two men will find other employment in the near future. There is a good chance they may sue you for wrongful dismissal.

3. Suspend Butch and Tom for two weeks without pay.

   This action would emphasize the company's displeasure with this type of behavior. You believe this action would send a strong message to all company employees.

   You estimate that costs incurred with this action will be up to $20,000. There is a slight probability that your company will be named in a lawsuit because of your stand. Given the strong action you took, it is unlikely you would lose the case.

4. Verbally warn the two men and place a note of reprimand in their personnel files stating any further problem in this area will result in their termination.

   You believe the banter was meant to be harmless. Once Butch and Tom recognize that some people find it unpleasant, they will stop. The two men are valued employees and would be difficult to replace.

   You estimate that costs incurred with this action will be up to $10,000. There is a slightly smaller probability of legal action than for Option #2, but an increased chance you will lose the case if a lawsuit is filed against your company.

5. Informally caution the two men.

   This approach would keep any disciplinary actions out of their personnel files and save the two men from public embarrassment. You are uncomfortable with taking stronger action before giving the men a chance to change their ways.

   You estimate no costs associated with this action. In fact, you think there could be some efficiencies achieved as people spend less time bantering. This could save up to $5,000 this quarter. You see this as only a temporary gain, expecting employees to return to joking around about topics other than sex.

   The lack of visible action will increase the chance of a lawsuit. If a suit is filed, you are likely to lose because you will be unable to show that you took any action to stop the men's behavior.

Enter the number of your decision on the Production and Finance screen.

APPENDIX H

INDUSTRY PERFORMANCE REPORTS

```
   EXAMPLE Industry   THRESHOLD Q 3 ACTUALS        DEMO 1 Company 1
File  Decision  Reports  Info  Print
```

QUARTER PERFORMANCE REPORT

COMP	SALES	PTS AWRD	INCOME	PTS AWRD	ROA	PTS AWRD	FORECAST ERRORS	PTS AWRD	OVERALL PTS	RANK
1.	604389	8	18240	30	1.92	17	1270	10*	65	3
2.	704704	10*	30700	50*	3.40	30*	1762	7	97	1
3.	715600	10*	20731	34	2.24	20	3706	3	67	2

```
   EXAMPLE Industry   THRESHOLD Q 3 ACTUALS        DEMO 1 Company 1
File  Decision  Reports  Info  Print
```

GAME TO DATE PERFORMANCE REPORT

COMP	SALES	PTS AWRD	INCOME	PTS AWRD	ROA	PTS AWRD	FORECAST ERRORS	PTS AWRD	OVERALL PTS	RANK
1.	2350232	9	58988	33	3.70	24	3656	9	75	3
2.	2550588	10*	89800	50*	4.65	30*	3229	10*	100	1
3.	2556791	10*	73866	41	4.14	27	5815	6	84	2

APPENDIX I

Quarter _____   *THRESHOLD*   Industry _____
Company _____

MARKETING

		Product 1	Product 2
Price		_____	_____
TV Ads	(Minutes)	_____	_____
Newspaper	(Column Inches)	_____	_____
Magazine Ads	(Pages)	_____	_____
Sales Forecast	(Units)	_____	_____

MARKETING RESEARCH

Price	_____	Product Quality	_____
TV Ads	_____	Units Sold	
Newspaper Ads	_____	Future Sales Potential (Qtr)	_____
Magazine Ads	_____		

PRODUCTION

		Product 1	Product 2
Buy Raw Materials (#)		_____	_____
Invest in Product Quality ($)		_____	_____
Units Produced (#)		_____	_____

Workers (#):	Hire	_____	Fire _____	Layoff _____
Plant Capacity:	Buy	_____	Sell _____	
Human Resource Development ($)		_____		

FINANCE

Short-Term Loan:	Request	_____	S T Investment: Deposit	_____
Mortgage	Request	_____	Withdrawal	_____
	Extra Payment	_____		

Dilemma Decision: _____

Appendix J
Threshold Flow Chart

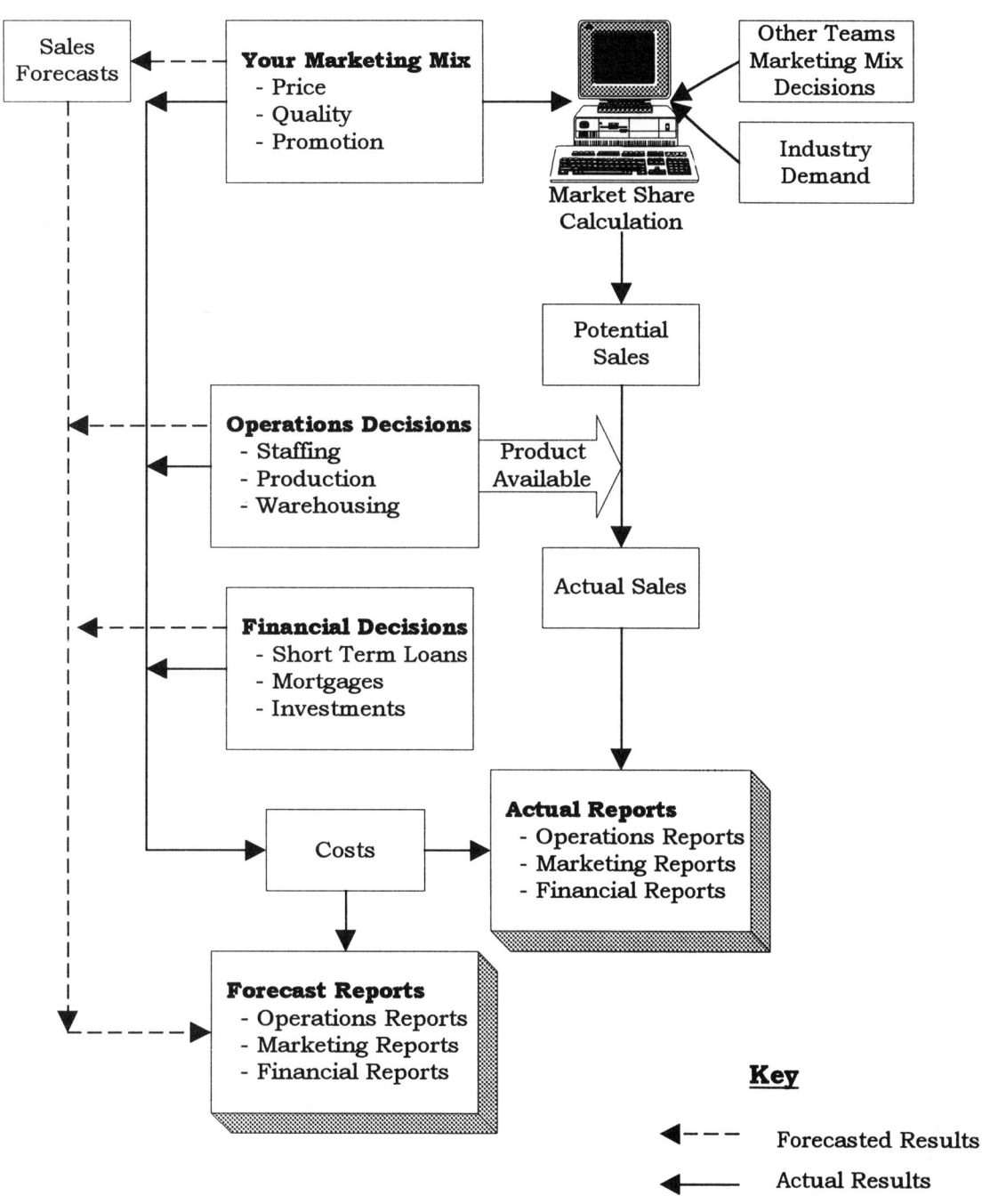

INDEX

Actual results   36, 46
Advertising (TV, newspaper, magazine)   5, 8, 14, 32, 44, 45, 47, 49, 55, 60, 63, 69
Assets   11, 66-68, 71

Backup disk   16, 17, 38, 39
Balance Sheet   16, 66-68, 71
Bulletin   32, 33
Business plan   43
Buy (purchase) plant capacity   52, 54
Buy (purchase) raw materials   31, 49, 52, 53, 54

Capacity: (manufacturing, plant)   10-12, 14, 49-54, 62, 63, 68, 70
Cash Flow Statement   56, 65, 67-71
Cash payments   56, 65, 69, 70
Cash receipts   68, 70
Change Password   26, 29
Change Company Name   26, 30
Company Name   19, 20, 26, 30
Computer system requirements   ii, 15
Control (controlling)   5-7, 10, 44, 50, 63, 64, 72
Copying disks   39
Correcting an error   40
Cost breakdowns   62, 63
Cost Parameters Report   33, 51, 57
Cost of Production Report   44, 51, 59, 61, 63, 64, 70
Current Assets   67
Current Liabilities   67, 68

Decision Menu   30, 41
Decision screens   13, 22-24, 36, 43, 44. 58
Dilemma   43, 56, 63
DOS Version   15, 18, 36,

Effective   5, 6, 9, 45, 46, 50
Efficient   5, 8, 44, 46, 53
Entering decisions   22
Error messages   28, 40, 48
Exiting the program   23, 30
Extra payment, mortgages   55

File Menu   19, 27
Finance Decisions   54
Finished goods inventory   49, 50, 58-60, 67, 70
Fire workers   49, 51, 52, 54, 60
Forecast reports (results)   35, 46
Future sales potential   48

Goals   5-10, 43, 48, 54, 64

Hard disk (drive)   15, 36 - 38
Hire workers   49, 51, 54
"Hot" keys   15, 16, 22, 24, 28, 30, 46
Human Resource Development   33, 49, 52, 53, 61

Icon   18, 37, 38
Industry Performance Report   71
Income Statement   56, 64-66, 69-71
Info menu   32
Inventory Report   58, 59, 69, 70

Labor   8, 12, 59-64, 70
Labor costs   51, 55, 62, 63, 70
Labor Report   25, 50, 60
Layoff workers   49, 52, 54, 60
Lead (leading)   5, 9
Liabilities   66-68
Limits, Marketing & Finance   25, 32, 33
Limits, Production   25, 33
Long-term Liabilities   67, 68
Lost sales   43, 50, 60

Magazine ads   45-48, 64
Manufacturing Capacity   10, 12, 14
Manufacturing cost   62, 64, 65
Market research   8, 13, 25, 44, 45, 47, 48, 63, 64
Marketing Decisions   44, 46, 47
Marketing & Finance Limits Report   25, 32
Menu Bar   15, 16, 19, 26 - 28, 46, 47, 57
Mission (Mission Statement)   6, 7, 43
Mistakes   21, 22, 36
Mortgage   12, 13, 54-56, 66, 68, 70
Moving from screen to screen   16, 23
Mouse, Using the   24

Navigating around *Threshold*   16
Newspaper ads   45-48, 64

Objectives   5
Owners' Equity   11, 68
Operations Reports   58, 64
Organize   5, 8
Overtime   12, 50

Password   21, 25, 29, 41
PgUp, PgDn   16, 24
Plan (planning)   1-3, 5-8, 15, 43, 46, 53, 54, 69, 70
Plant capacity   11, 31, 49-54, 63, 68, 70
Policies   5-7, 43, 53
Production costs   61, 62
Program failure   40

Program Manager   18, 19, 37, 38
Price   8, 22, 36, 43-50, 66
Print (All Pages, Current Screen, Decisions, Selected Screens)   34, 35
Print menu   33, 57
Product quality   7, 8, 13, 45-50, 54, 70
Production costs   61, 62
Production decision   49, 53, 54
Production Limits Report   25, 33
Production workers   12, 31, 49, 51-53, 63
Points Awarded (PTS AWRD)   71, 72

Quality   5, 7, 8, 13, 31, 43-50, 54, 61, 70
Quantity discounts, raw materials   49

Raw Material Inventory   49, 50, 58, 59, 62, 67, 70
Raw Material shortages   49
Reports menu   31
Re-process   17, 41
Return on Assets (ROA)   71, 72
Run screen   19

Safety stock   8, 10, 49
Sales forecast   22, 35-36, 43-47, 71, 72
Sales potential   48
Saving decisions   16, 23, 30, 34, 40
Select Quarter   28, 31, 41, 58
Sell plant capacity   52-54
Selling and Administrative Expense Report   63, 66
Setup instructions (Setting up)   18
Short-term loan   12, 13, 46, 54-56, 66, 68, 70, 71
Short-term investment   54-56, 66-68, 70
Staff (staffing)   5, 8, 12, 52, 63, 64, 70
Strategy (strategies)   5, 7, 8, 13, 14, 43, 44, 48, 49, 52
System failure   40

Tips   2
Total Assets   67, 68, 71
Training (Human Resource Development)   31, 53, 60
Trouble shooting   40
Turnover, worker   12, 13, 52
TV ads   46-48

Unit cost   12, 59, 60, 62, 63
Units produced   50, 51, 54
Units sold   48

Viruses   18, 40

Windows version   15, 16, 18, 19, 37-39
Workers (hire, fire, layoff, turnover)   12, 13, 49, 51, 52, 54, 60

YOU SHOULD CAREFULLY READ THE TERMS AND CONDITIONS BEFORE USING THE DISKETTE PACKAGE. USING THIS DISKETTE PACKAGE INDICATES YOUR ACCEPTANCE OF THESE TERMS AND CONDITIONS.

Prentice-Hall, Inc. provides this program and licenses its use. You assume responsibility for the selection of the program to achieve your intended results, and for the installation, use, and results obtained from the program. This license extends only to use of the program in the United States or countries in which the program is marketed by authorized distributors.

LICENSE GRANT
You hereby accept a nonexclusive, nontransferable, permanent license to install and use the program ON A SINGLE COMPUTER at any given time. You may copy the program solely for backup or archival purposes in support of your use of the program on the single computer. You may not modify, translate, disassemble, decompile, or reverse engineer the program, in whole or in part.

TERM
The License is effective until terminated. Prentice-Hall, Inc. reserves the right to terminate this License automatically if any provision of the License is violated. You may terminate the License at any time. To terminate this License, you must return the program, including documentation, along with a written warranty stating that all copies in your possession have been returned or destroyed.

LIMITED WARRANTY
THE PROGRAM IS PROVIDED "AS IS" WITHOUT WARRANTY OF ANY KIND, EITHER EXPRESSED OR IMPLIED, INCLUDING, BUT NOT LIMITED TO, THE IMPLIED WARRANTIES OR MERCHANTABILITY AND FITNESS FOR A PARTICULAR PURPOSE. THE ENTIRE RISK AS TO THE QUALITY AND PERFORMANCE OF THE PROGRAM IS WITH YOU. SHOULD THE PROGRAM PROVE DEFECTIVE, YOU (AND NOT PRENTICE-HALL, INC. OR ANY AUTHORIZED DEALER) ASSUME THE ENTIRE COST OF ALL NECESSARY SERVICING, REPAIR, OR CORRECTION. NO ORAL OR WRITTEN INFORMATION OR ADVICE GIVEN BY PRENTICE-HALL, INC., ITS DEALERS, DISTRIBUTORS, OR AGENTS SHALL CREATE A WARRANTY OR INCREASE THE SCOPE OF THIS WARRANTY.

SOME STATES DO NOT ALLOW THE EXCLUSION OF IMPLIED WARRANTIES, SO THE ABOVE EXCLUSION MAY NOT APPLY TO YOU. THIS WARRANTY GIVES YOU SPECIFIC LEGAL RIGHTS AND YOU MAY ALSO HAVE OTHER LEGAL RIGHTS THAT VARY FROM STATE TO STATE.

Prentice-Hall, Inc. does not warrant that the functions contained in the program will meet your requirements or that the operation of the program will be uninterrupted or error-free.

However, Prentice-Hall, Inc. warrants the diskette(s) on which the program is furnished to be free from defects in material and workmanship under normal use for a period of ninety (90) days from the date of delivery to you as evidenced by a copy of your receipt.

The program should not be relied on as the sole basis to solve a problem whose incorrect solution could result in injury to person or property. If the program is employed in such a manner, it is at the user's own risk and Prentice-Hall, Inc. explicitly disclaims all liability for such misuse.

LIMITATION OF REMEDIES
Prentice-Hall, Inc.'s entire liability and your exclusive remedy shall be:
1. the replacement of any diskette not meeting Prentice-Hall, Inc.'s "LIMITED WARRANTY" and that is returned to Prentice-Hall, or
2. if Prentice-Hall is unable to deliver a replacement diskette that is free of defects in materials or workmanship, you may terminate this agreement by returning the program.

IN NO EVENT WILL PRENTICE-HALL, INC. BE LIABLE TO YOU FOR ANY DAMAGES, INCLUDING ANY LOST PROFITS, LOST SAVINGS, OR OTHER INCIDENTAL OR CONSEQUENTIAL DAMAGES ARISING OUT OF THE USE OR INABILITY TO USE SUCH PROGRAM EVEN IF PRENTICE-HALL, INC. OR AN AUTHORIZED DISTRIBUTOR HAS BEEN ADVISED OF THE POSSIBILITY OF SUCH DAMAGES, OR FOR ANY CLAIM BY ANY OTHER PARTY.

SOME STATES DO NOT ALLOW FOR THE LIMITATION OR EXCLUSION OF LIABILITY FOR INCIDENTAL OR CONSEQUENTIAL DAMAGES, SO THE ABOVE LIMITATION OR EXCLUSION MAY NOT APPLY TO YOU.

GENERAL
You may not sublicense, assign, or transfer the license of the program. Any attempt to sublicense, assign or transfer any of the rights, duties, or obligations hereunder is void.

This Agreement will be governed by the laws of the State of New York.

Should you have any questions concerning this Agreement, you may contact Prentice-Hall, Inc. by writing to:
Director of New Media
Higher Education Division
Prentice-Hall, Inc.
1 Lake Street
Upper Saddle River, NJ 07458

Should you have any questions concerning technical support, you may write to:
New Media Production
Higher Education Division
Prentice-Hall, Inc.
1 Lake Street
Upper Saddle River, NJ 07458

YOU ACKNOWLEDGE THAT YOU HAVE READ THIS AGREEMENT, UNDERSTAND IT, AND AGREE TO BE BOUND BY ITS TERMS AND CONDITIONS. YOU FURTHER AGREE THAT IT IS THE COMPLETE AND EXCLUSIVE STATEMENT OF THE AGREEMENT BETWEEN US THAT SUPERSEDES ANY PROPOSAL OR PRIOR AGREEMENT, ORAL OR WRITTEN, AND ANY OTHER COMMUNICATIONS BETWEEN US RELATING TO THE SUBJECT MATTER OF THIS AGREEMENT.

THE WHO'S BUYING SERIES
BY THE NEW STRATEGIST EDITORS

Who's Buying Executive Summary of Household Spending

2nd EDITION

New Strategist Publications, Inc.
P.O. Box 242, Ithaca, New York 14851
800/848-0842; 607/273-0913
www.newstrategist.com

Copyright 2006. NEW STRATEGIST PUBLICATIONS, INC.

All rights reserved.

No part of this book may be reproduced, stored in a retrieval system, or transmitted in any form or by any means, electronic, mechanical, photocopying, microfilming, recording, or otherwise without written permission from the Publisher.

ISBN 978-1-933588-22-3
ISSN 1933-2009

Printed in the United States of America